LOVE AND PARADOX

A collection of poems

JOSEPH OVWEMUVWOSE

This page is intentionally left blank

Copyright © 2023 Joseph Ovwemuvwose

Joseph Ovwemuvwose
Imperial College London
South Kensington Campus
London SW7 2AZ, UK
tel: +44(0)2075895111
J.ovwemuvwose22@imperial.ac.uk
j.ovwemuvwose@emmu.co.uk
https://www.emmu.co.uk
https://www.imperial.ac.uk/people/j.ovwemuvwose22

All right reserved. No portion of this book may be reproduced, stored in a retrieval system, or transmitted, in any form or by any means without the prior permission in writing of the author. However, excerpts can be taken from this book for personal and educational purposes provided the author is duly cited.

Dedication

Dedicated to everyone protecting the freedom to hold constructive conversations.

Contents

Dedication
Contents
Prologue — 1

Part One: Nature and Wellbeing — 3

The Beach Beckons — 4
Emil and the Beach — 6
Behold the Sea — 12
Precious Pearl — 14
The Coronation — 17
The Call of Dawn — 20
Dear Summer — 22
Peaks and Valleys — 25
Transition — 28

Part Two: Love and Inspiration — 31

Echoes of the Heart — 32
Uncertainty and Certainty — 36
I Tried — 37
Skills and Bills — 39
Significant Figures — 42
The Foolish Farmer — 46
Please Pause — 48

The Road I Took	51
Dare to Dive	56
Thorns and Fragrance	59
Broken Tile	61
Love and Paradox	64
The Edge of Grief	69

Part Three: Society and Politics   73

At the City Centre	74
Wine	77
The Politician's Pledge	79
Mad House	83
The Days of Death	85
The Dead Head	90
Neurons and Neutrophils	94
The Malleability of Modernity	97
The Ballot and the Bullet	102
On Strange Tongue	105
The Twitter Trender	107
The Mad Maid	109
The Brand Paradox	111
The Needy and the Greedy	114

The Hot Tripod	118
Rasps of Reeds	121
I had a Dream	124
How the World Works	127
Boobs and Butts	129

Part Four: Religion and Philosophy 134

The Sermonizing of Semen	135
Let us Prey	138
The God Maker	140
The Fortunes of Fiction	143
The Manipulation of Man	146
The Deadly Tome	149
The Death of the Dead	155
Foes and Friends	159

Part Five: Race and Diversity 163

The Black Man's Nod	164
Black and Whitening	165
Bents and Straights	168
Black and White	171
Dusk and Dawn	174
Oceans and Deserts	180

Me and My Hair	188
Ajekpako and Ajebota	190
Wild White West	193
Compressive Ambivalence	197

About the Author 202

Prologue

The following poems are the musings of my mind. They give life and visibility to my thoughts. The verses cover most of the things I care about. Like every work of art, their interpretations are not cast in stone. You can interpret them however you chose, as long as your motives are solely driven by an appreciation of the liberty and complex beauty of art. Many of the matters discussed in the verses are neutral and enjoyable and they are constructed on various themes. I assure every reader that my utmost desire is to share some bits of my life. If by reading my poems your thoughts, perceptions and leanings are tickled, I will be the most excited and grateful. My purpose of making this collection available is so that you can read, enjoy, question and share, and if it interests you to discuss a line, a verse, or a poem, please do reach me by my email.

JOSEPH OVWEMUVWOSE

Part One: Nature and Wellbeing

The Beach Beckons
Emil and the Beach
Behold the Sea
Precious Pearl
The Coronation
The Call of Dawn
Dear Summer
Peaks and Valleys
Transition

JOSEPH OVWEMUVWOSE

The Beach Beckons

I have been to beaches on many occasions, not once have I seen a sad face by the waters.

I gaze upon the sea from the shore.
My sight ended but not the sea, nor its waters.
I stood at the beginning of my horizon,
Its end thereof no man can tell.
This speaks to me of endless prospects.

Can I retain my sadness at the beach?
I have been to beaches, not a few.
And I have walked by the water,
In more occasions than one.
All I saw was ebullience, friendly funs,
Smiles and laughter in the water of salt.
Humanity of all ages, faith, faces and race,
Swimming to fortify their muscles and mind.
For to go in the deep of the water is bravery,
And to swim against the tides is courage.

I have been to many beaches,
And in many occasions than one

LOVE AND PARADOX

Not once did I see a sad face, ever.
Nor a mother's sigh or a child's cry.
The waves are loved by all,
The breeze on the water is bliss.
Salty water dissolves distress,
At the dip of the feet.
The coming waves brings delight,
Bearing away the sorrows of men,
As it recedes.
Misdemeanour and folly of friends is fun,
Invoking gleeful laughter by the water.

Falling asleep by the beach,
Need no sweet dreams,
For the spirit of the seaside,
Caressing the skin, tasty enough,
The delicious sound of the waves,
Kissing the ears, fresh air, airy.
This mixture, a luscious reality,
More pleasant than all pleasing dreams.

JOSEPH OVWEMUVWOSE

Emil and the Beach

At the beach all the elements of life converge, and where the elements are gathered, there is fullness of joy.

If the sea were a god,
The beach a goddess,
Emil would be the priestess.
Yet she prefers to be a humble stone,
By the seaside.
Her bothersome ways, immeasurable,
To go to the beach, to sit and watch.
'Go with a book to read,
Or a jotter and a pen,' she says.
She drove me mad persistently.
I see no practical use for the beach,
I listened, went, and sat on a stone.
I picked my pen and began a poem.
It's for her I write.

The beach in my eyes transformed anew,
A lens that paints its practical view.
The beach is a place of positive vibes.
Its frequency hangs at the edge of bliss.

Old and young, men and women,
The beach unites all in happiness.

When the pressure of life overwhelms,
Your fortune is great if it's in summer,
And you live not far away from the seaside.
Go there and open your heart to the breeze,
Let it carry away your pressures in its train.
And leave your heart refreshed, free of pains.
As the salty water cleanses your soul,
In harmony with the tides' constant roll.

If by grace you have no fear of water,
Take a plunge, swim a while, against
And with the tides.
Allow the tides to bear away your strains,
Imbuing your bare heart with elated gains.
If the water be cold, the better it shall be,
For in dipping your body in the cold water,
As the sun burns your skin,
There is a clash of energies,
The warm and the uncaring,
The sunshine and the chilling water,

Mingling and fighting for a place
In your body, spirit and soul.
This thermal war rouses the senses,
Turning dark gloom into joyful grace.

The soothing sound of the waves,
Iteratively strikes the sandy seaside,
That comes at regular intervals,
Calms the mind like nothing else.
To get into the rhythm of your being,
Take a stony seat by the seashore,
And listen to the splashes come and go.

The beach imparts wisdom profound,
Teaching that what once goes around,
Shall return in due course,
Like life's crest and trough's discourse.
The left and right, the peak and valley,
They are two sides of a whole.
The waves that have receded,
Will surely return in due time.
If by chance of circumstances,
You are left crestfallen,
Remember the waves' crest shall rise.

At the beach, breath in, breath out.
Let the salty steam fill your lungs.
It kills all germ, in mind and body.
Let the fresh air cuddle you.
Allow it to caress you like a lover does.
This will bless you with unending rapture.

For every sense the beach has a treat.
Let the sand marry your bare feet,
And let its grains remind you of infinity,
Let your eyes behold the endless water,
And let that retell your inner eyes,
Of endless opportunities,
Let the fresh air soar into your nostrils,
Let that fondle your sense of smell,
As it reminds you of unboundedness,
Taste the tingly taste of the water's brine,
A reminder that you are connected to the sea,
By the salt-essence of water, bones and blood line.

Visit the beach with someone dear,
Shared euphoria amplifies cheer,

Life and joy, when embraced with others,
Blossom manifold, in a magnified order.

Now Emil, the beach, and I, we won,
The beach heals, lifts, and clears,
In its embrace, broken hearts find sun,
A formidable healing it engineers.

When else you are down,
Take a walk by the beach,
If you are still down,
Walk barefooted,
If you are still down,
Plunge into the water and swim,
If you are still down, wait and enjoy
The sunset by the beach,
If you are still down, wait and watch
The stars by the beach,
This is a powerful remedy,
If you can say a prayer,
Healing is on the way.

Now the beach is my companion,
I will go as often as I can,

For at the beach lies
The harmony of the elements:
Earth, water, air, and sun.
And where all the elements are gathered,
There is fullness of life,
And where there is fullness of life,
There is fullness of joy.

JOSEPH OVWEMUVWOSE

Behold the Sea

The sea teaches me of endless possibilities.

Here I am beholding the sea,
Its whole content I couldn't see.
As for the water within it,
No man's measurement is fit.

Oh, you boundless water body,
What is the origin of your story?
Are you just a product of atomic reaction,
Or the outcome of the fingers of creation?

Just looking over you,
I learnt some lessons too.
Your vastness tells of endless possibility,
At the reach of the hands of responsibility.

As the breeze caress its surface,
It came rushing to the coastal face.
Earth, water and air, life's elements.
Connect without disagreement.
Oh dear sea, I see you.

And I take a part of you with me.
And you have always lived with me too.
I drink you every week in my tea.

JOSEPH OVWEMUVWOSE

Precious Pearl

They who carry precious pearl should run with care.

Few months ago,
I set myself on the go,
On my way to the seashore.
Others have been there before,
So I was told,
Searching for gold.

I packed my bag,
And tucked in some rag,
So I could dig in the mud,
Without the fear of being mugged.

And there I was, searching and digging,
Night and day without tiring,
Alas! All I saw were granite and stones.
A lot of them would not leave me alone,
No matter how hard I tried to say no,
We all our needs do know.
The next day, I packed my bag,
And tucked in some rag,

So I could dig in the sand,
Perhaps I might find,
That which I seek.

There it's, a precious pearl,
A gem of inestimable value,
Worthy beyond what I can tell.
I asked her, 'Is that you?'

With both hands I picked her,
With the care for a golden egg,
And put her in my bag,
And began my walk back home,
At a time, I began to run.
Full of excitement and glee.

Unknown to me,
That they who carry precious pearl,
Shouldn't run with too much excitement,
For gems like golden eggs,
Could fall and break.
And now I'm back home,
My bag is empty,
My precious pearl had leaked.

It fell on the way.
And my heart is broken.
Here I'm lain on my bed,

In the place of sleep tears,
In the place of rest rolling,
I can't go back to the seashore,
Precious pearls are very rare,
And the journey is so far.

I shall search the highway,
I shall search the waterway,
I shall wait in patience,
And I shall pray,
Someday, not so far from today,
My precious pearl shall come,
But until then,
I shall hope, believe and be kind.

The Coronation

Nature when disrespected has a way of reacting.

The tale was told of a countryside nearby,
When some distressed creatures gathered with agonizing sighs.
Mothers came with offspring letting out deafening cries.

'They are killing us and wiping us from the face of the universe.'
They shouted while they deliberated and conversed.
'Their seeds to us from the beginning have always been perverse.

We got here many days before their forefathers arrived.
We are generous enough to give them spaces in which to thrive,
We give them all they need to survive.

We give them homes, from thatch houses to mansions of luxury,
We clothe them with wool and keep them from going hungry,
Yet, their deeds to us everywhere have always been extortionary.

What shall we do to these selfish creatures,
Who had toppled the ecosystem architecture,
And force us into an imbalanced indenture?'

That was the matter they were there to examine.
'Rain please cease to be and let there be grievous famine.'
They also pleaded with the sun to never, ever shine.

The sons of men have insight, hindsight and foresight,
They have irrigation for rain and million facilities for light.'

This objection came from their elites.

Thus, that day, they could not come to an agreeable conclusion.
And they told themselves, 'Let's postpone the coronation,
Until we can fathom an assault that will defy all their inventions.'

JOSEPH OVWEMUVWOSE

The Call of Dawn

Mother says the first crow of the cock in the morning is our call to duty.

All that's needed is an adequate sleep,
And not just for routine to keep.
But a response of rest to labour.
Slumber is not a proof of productivity,
I've worked hard, I shall yet be engaged in profitable endeavours.

That I indulge in sleep inconsistencies,
Is not the definition of me at my best.
These are unprecedented times,
Of course, I'm not making any excuse.
I've never slept beyond the call of duties,
And to bury my head beneath the pillow
And duvet while duty calls is irresponsibility.
You're right,
Morning has at its grip,
The invitation to wakefulness.
And because I admire Jesus,
He woke early before dawn,

Went to a solitary place for prayer.

Men should be awake in the morning,
When the crow of the cock
Signals the break of another day,
Dawn calls, responsible men should respond.

JOSEPH OVWEMUVWOSE

Dear Summer

Summer smiles while we await winter's weeping.

I am writing to you Miss Summer.
You remember the day we met,
At the Musee de Fabre,
In the Southern France city of Montpellier?
You were all smiles and delight.
You told me of the beautiful petals
That were springing forth,
Very vibrant in the garden of green.
When I complained of the sunny heat,
You chided me a bit lovely,
And reminded me of your younger sister,
Who was shopping for blankets at
Odeyssium,
And that when she returns,
I would wish I never whine of your warmth.

Summer and I had a very warm date.
We walked through London hand in hand.
We kissed as often as we could,
We even sang along the birds in the park.

The grasses were swanky underneath our feet,
The sepals, petals, leaves, and pollens
Were there to witness our affection.

When we got home,
She told me to open all my windows.
I did as she advised,
The breeze that came was warm-hearted,
She loved to drink water as much as I.
But I had to make lemonade,
She didn't care about my lemonade and wine.
'A cup of smoothie and a glass of water would do.' She said.

What I loved the most about her,
The brightness and beauty of her beam.
And when she was about leaving,
I held her hand and told her to stay a while,
But she pleaded to go.
Because in her home
Both sisters can't be home at once.
As she drove off in her car,

JOSEPH OVWEMUVWOSE

My brain and heart joined my eyes
In the feast of loss and grief.
There were drops of liquid,
Tears from my eyes,
And the eyes of the sky.

Peaks and Valleys

Interacting with all the elements of nature has a way of making life fulfilling.

While trees stand behind the awesome mountain,
Among the pines planted in heights of windy plane,
I walked beneath their shadows in sunset,
As light of dusk tears away his canopy skirt.
I wore my glasses to shield my eyes from its glares.
For although it's setting, yet it bites with stares.

My journey to the Transylvania mountains,
A region that has less attention gain,
Buried beneath the shadows of false stories.
Told by men who wear broken, tainted glasses.
I plan to bring this place to a global light,
That its narrative would be set aright.
The beauties of its planes be made plain,
For who have gone before to go again.

I picked the pine exudates and cones.
When pines bleed, their blood is myrrh.
I smelt them with noses standing on stones.
I walked through paths that feet wear,
As men hiked underneath canopies
Over slippery soil soiled by sole of shoes
Of those traveling rugged terrain with buddies,
As they walked the trails, hands in hand, two by two.

I sat upon cut and fallen long soggy logs.
They lay there sleeping and slipping away.
Rotted by the dying deeds of liquified fogs.
Roots standing while leaves their place stay.
We cracked rock with rocks and pebble with stones.
Climbing mountains and counting the years of trees,
By the circular rings of their marrows and bones.
And ears for the twisted dances and buzzes of bees.
Water ruptures hard rock and walked by,

Running down brooks beside grey gravels,
Above the green mountain greying sky,
Planned pine-needle-fingered my travel.

Here I pitched my tent by the stream.
My feet hanging over faeces-fed grasses,
By goats, sheep and cows, nuns of dreams,
Hope dashed, by the night grips of tasses.

I rested my back on a rocky sack in a weak tent.
By the stream in a deadly cold and ill-fated night.
That was the only pain that blighted my ascent,
To that peak that serves the eye a dignified sight.

Transition

To change for good is wisdom. Adaptability is a necessity for advancement.

Flying, swimming, walking and running,
She does that in all the elements.
Whether the weather is foul or clement.
She is never stopped from moving.
Yea! Progress, land, air and sea,
Willingness is all that's key.

Today I watched and learned my lessons.
Survival, evolution, adaptability, the Red Queen.
Progress, forward, change, this is transition.
The duck, conqueror of all of nature,
Draws my unreserved admiration,
As my imagination beholds the future.

She pulls herself from the water,
And swam the air with her wing.
Water, land and air are the same to her.
Her webbed feet, strong feathers keep singing,

Across space and planes with graceful gliding,
And she sauntered farther and further.

There I was by the lake side,
Just watching her live her life,
Dominating the elements with ease.
All state conquered; gas, liquid and solid,
To me she reigns in the beasts' kingdom.
Not eagle, lion nor parrot with their strength and beauty.
I'll give her the crown without a second thought.

While I watched, I got some lease,
Of what I could do to conquer the world.
To change for good is wisdom.
Adaptability will keep the dream unfurled.
To conquer all land, race and gender,
Growth, the progressive kind,
Should be held tenaciously.
While I maintain my elegant plume,
 And preserve my inner core.

Part Two: Love and Inspiration

Echoes of the Heart
Uncertainty and Certainty
I Tried
Skills and Bills
Significant Figures
The Foolish Farmer
Please Pause
The Road I Took
Dare to Dive
Thorns and Fragrance
Love and Paradox
The Edge of Grief

JOSEPH OVWEMUVWOSE

Echoes of the Heart

The world like a mirror reflects the intents of our hearts.

Every surface interacts with the rays,
That beam from the sun at the break of day.
Things dull and lustrous,
Things rough and smooth,
Things straight and crooked,
Gorgeous glimmers of sunlight,
Hits every spot at a time on earth.

Things dark reflect lesser light,
Things shaggy roughen the rays,
Things serpentine twist the beams,
What the eyes see as an object,
Is what the object is.
Light is neutrally colourful,
When it is natural,
Its smiles amplify the
essence of things and beings.
It only reveals what is.
Walking through the garden,
We saw flowers; blue, green,

Yellow, red, pink, white and more.
They are what they are,
They are seen the way they are,
By their meeting with illumination,
They're taken from their shroud,
And their core is revealed.

Life like light,
Is circumstantially neutral.
In many instances I may say,
When its beams of all sorts,
Hit us as they often do,
Whether we smile with hope,
Or weep with despair,
Whether we trust in faith,
Or worry in doubt,
Is a product of our inner being.

She places a lavender flower,
Held in flawless fingers,
Over the still and clean water
In that pool,
There is the reflection of the tender fingers,
Holding the elegant flowers,

In the exact shape and dimension,
Life like reflection.
Gives us what we give it.

Then I spoke across the park,
What I said hits a surface,
And back it came as an echo.
The edict of planting and harvesting,
Still hold whether we say so or no.
We hear the echo of the ear,
We see the echo of the eyes.

What about the echo of the heart?
Why not think about the echo of the mind,
And the enactment of life's attraction?
Which in life opposes that of magnets.
Unlike the poles, life attracts its like.
Why not place some lovely lavender
Over a clear pool?
It's certain, you'll get back lavender.
Life like an echo,
Reflects our liberality.
Let the heart send out something sublime,
It will receive the echoes of beauty.

If not every time, most of the time.

JOSEPH OVWEMUVWOSE

Uncertainty and Certainty

It is alright if things are messy every now and then.

My mind is clouded,
I don't know what I'm seeing,
The future is vague.

I'm not here nor there,
But when I come looking for me,
I'll be here or there.

I Tried

You can only do your best.

I tried to convince them,
That I am a decent Nigerian,
But they didn't believe me.
So, I walked away.

I tried to convince them,
That I am a brilliant black man,
But they didn't believe me.
So, I walked away.

I tried to convince them,
That I am a trustworthy person,
But they didn't believe me.
So, I walked away.

I tried to convince them,
That I don't tell lies.
But they didn't believe me.
So, I walked away.

I tried to convince them,
That I really love them,
But they didn't believe me.
So, I walked away.

I tried to convince them,
That I have very great talents,
But they didn't believe me.
So, I walked away.

I tried to convince them,
That I have a great future,
But they didn't believe me.
So, I walked away.

LOVE AND PARADOX

Skills and Bills

*There are those born on the moon for life
condemned them to do things differently if
they must thrive, they are aliens.*

Twice I've been told by friends so dear,
That I am a descendant of the moon.
For my social life is weird and strange.
And to shave my beards,
Is to court acne and facial aches.

My father fathered me when he died.
His grey hair and wrinkled hands,
Caressed my infant brow.
As he came so he went.

And the basics became my needs.
Survival and struggle, I've got to feed,
And seeing beyond today, tomorrow says read.

When the moon birthed me,
The stars were not silvery.

And the spoon I had was earthen,
And it broke before I could use it.

The sinewy arms of my mother held me,
And her wrinkled smiles taught me to swim,
Against the river tide and life flow.
And here I stand, left to the elements.

To live or die, what do you chose?
To lay and decay, is that a fate preferred?
No, I said, no and again, I said no!
Tomorrow beacons with a bright sun,
Let's go and see what it holds.

And so the journey began.
I did what I did, not what they did.
And the world became a strange place.
And I am an alien, birthed by the moon.

I laboured and learned,
Doing little but much.
When they played the video game,
I laboured with the time on jobs that pay.
And because I have to solely pay the bills,

The time I've I spent on the needed skills.
For by it I can master my destiny.

JOSEPH OVWEMUVWOSE

Significant Figures

Once in a while men need the shoulder of a giant to stand on.

I was in London the other day,
I went by train and alighted at
The Westminster Station.
I walked across the bridge,
That noble London bridge,
That runs over the Thame.

I went through to Victoria.
I looked around at the architecture,
The edifices are marvelously gigantic.
Government houses, business structures,
Hospitals, Hotels, offices, and parking lot,
Here, the ancient meets the modern.
It is the fusion of the old and the new.

Beauty stared at me from the concretes,
It is reflected here and there in glasses.
Trees and flowers, on the ground and rooftops,
People, birds, cars, buses and, bicycles,

Shoppers, and daters and sellers,
Onlookers, protesters, policemen and passers bye,
All mingling in fluid-peaceful isolation.

And there it is,
The Westminster Abbey,
An old church in an ancient city.
One thing kept me puzzled while I looked,
The overly complex grandeur of this polis.
How can it be so old and yet so new?
Construction works are ongoing,
They have built and they are building,
Buildings on top of buildings,
Structures upon structures.

At the centre of this soupy city,
The melting pot for all the world,
Are statues of men who wrote world history.
They stole my admiration right from birth.
Standing out to me were,
Nelson Mandela of South Africa,
Mahatma Gandhi of India,
And Winston Churchill of England.

I wanted to hug them,
Or perhaps sit at their feet,
But the statues are so large.
And they're lifted on platforms so high,
With my phone I took their photograph,
While I looked around for some epitaph.
But these are not gravestones,
They are platforms of reminder,
To tell men that noble deeds,
Do outlive the doers.
I took more selfie,
They stood as my background.

While I walked around, I contemplated,
The single thread that tied these three,
Churchill is a man of an iron will,
Gandhi is a man of unrelenting tenacity,
And Nelson is a man of solid resolve.

Nelson was willing to sacrifice for his cause,
Mahatma was determined to stay his cause,
And Winston believed in his cause.
These men were selfless, fearless and forgiving,

They held to the truth and stuck it through,
They won their enemies albeit non-violently.

They stood alone many a time,
They cried alone many a time,
They fought tyrants and their armies,
Some believed in the equality of all,
And together in a chorus they told me,
"You could be greater than we are."

And here they are standing at the centre of the world.
They're long dead and yet living, talking and inspiring.
Their works, words and books are motivational anchors.
And they have touched me more than many living friends.
I stood afar and took a last look at them,
And I seem to hear them say to me in one accord,
"We are the Significant Figures,
What can you do to be one of us?"

JOSEPH OVWEMUVWOSE

The Foolish Farmer

A problem not solved at the root, is not solved at all.

That foolish farmer
Presiding over his withering crops,
His goats ate some and drank from the pool.
There in the green water are algae,
Some are deadly and the goats died.
The cows ate in the pasture,
In the grasses are mushrooms-deadly.
The cows died.
The crops are withering,
The stream is running dry.

The foolish farmer
Presiding over his failing farm,
Traveled across town.
Two miles, three miles, a lot of miles.
He came to a field of flocks,
Full of green grasses and healthy herds.
"This farmer is great but I'm greater."

He patted his breast.
The crops are luxuriant,
The leaves open to the sun,
They're eating and growing.
They're healthy.

The foolish farmer having looked at
 This flourishing farm,
Went home to labour afresh.
"I will plant more crops there,
I'll buy more flocks here,
I will've a greater herd next year"
These crops died,
And the flocks died.
And he died.

He was dumb,
He was blind,
He was deaf,
And his brain was dead.
The foolish farmer was
A living dead man who died.

Please Pause

At times it is good to just stop.

While I reflect on the pains of the lockdown,
In this very, very strange and metallic town.
I began to envisage another kind of beauty,
Which comes in moments of tranquility.
When you have a conversation with you.
And you ask yourself; "What should I do?"
When you see that you've been on the run,
And not even bordering to stop for some fun.
That is why a time to stop on your course,
Could really be a pretty pause.

Today I said to myself while walking home,
"Many a time you have pored over many tomes.
What are those things you have foregone,
Just so you can focus on achieving your ambition?"
And here came the interesting list;

An emotional moment of a passionate kiss,
The comfort, tenderness and warmth of her hug,
An opportunity to explore the forest's bugs,
And contemplate the very beauty of nature.
And later, dance the dance of the matured.
I have to consider this course,
Because I was in the midst of a pretty pause.

Everyone, everywhere and every time,
Has been a very part of this modern crime.
"I don't think I have time, I'm very busy."
And we always fail to take life easy.
We jump from pillars to poles and back again,
And many a time we come down with pains.
And we don't border to just lay and rest,
Because we are never satisfied with our best.
And then something and maybe someone saw us,
And I know they sent the pretty pause.

Pause is wise,
Because it makes one to stop and think.
Pause is nice,
Because it helps one to step back.
Pause is helpful,
Because it enables one to listen.
Pause is strengthening,
Because it makes some to rest.
Pause is refreshing,
Because it makes one to start again.

Whatever you do, just pause before, during and after.
Then continue because pause is pretty.

The Road I Took

When the direction is not clear I follow my heart.

Every road, dirt, or paved calls unto a journey,
Every journey, brief or lengthy calls unto life,
Life whether worthy with gold and goods or vain with vices and vitriol calls unto time in all its kits.
Here time is pleased to bow in obeisance to eternity.
I am given a century or less on this path,
Ten decades yes, but very brief still.
While we walk this part of eternity, we know not what lies ahead.
That is for the future to decide.
But it is ours to choose the road we must take.

I passed through the past a few seconds ago,

While coming here I passed narrow and wide ways,
I saw people ugly and beautiful,
I bathed in the rain and shine,
I almost drown in floods and thirst to death in deserts.
The *Iroko* in the rainforest gave me cool shades,
The itchy savanna shrubs flustered me a great deal,
My skin is covered with scars of wounds,
And tattoos of triumph.

My brain is full of the handwritings of hurts and healings.
On my way I met two bridges, one reminds of afflictions,
So, I destroyed it for my brain to forget its hurts,
For to reflects on one's hurt is to feel the pain again.
The second bridge on the highway of benevolence I repaired.

It leads the memory to hearts of gold and victories on past battlefields and playgrounds.
And that is on the road I'll always take.

I am on my way to tomorrow, sometime away from now. It is on its way towards me.
The future is always on its way.
If I make a list of events for coming days, and say a prayer,
Talk about them and rehearse the plans.
This is all I could do and then wrap them in hope.
I could say to my tomorrow," Please come this way."
It may reply, "I am going that other route, it suits me more."
If I look ahead at it and my eyes behold a sunny sky,
But decide to go along with an umbrella as well as sunglasses,
That would be walking on the way with both eyes opened.
Whether tomorrow goes north or south,

JOSEPH OVWEMUVWOSE

The road I will take is the way my heart commands.

Here I am standing at a junction,
On my way to my unknown destination,
A point at which four roads meet.
One goes ahead of me, one goes to my left,
One to the right and the last goes the way I came.

Oh friends! How do you choose the way to the unknown, on a sunny day, so hot and dry that your skin burns, and you are thirsty to death?
I have a destination in mind that nobody knows,
And I do not know how to get there.
How do you decide the road to take
At a junction of four roads?
I listened to the wind, I looked to the sun,
I listened to the birds sing,
I watched the trees and grasses sway,
But none of these knows the way.

Then I listened to my heart,
It revealed a certain way pointing a finger unseen,
And the way my heart pointed was the road I took.

JOSEPH OVWEMUVWOSE

Dare to Dive

You never know what you could accomplish until you try.

The bruit like breeze
Blows about never ceased.
Putting pebbles on zinc.
Not be bothered to think
Upon whose house they land.
Daily it comes in bands,
It whispered into my ear,
The tale of a mysterious sea afar.

No joke it seems,
A thousand had the dream,
They come and go to tell a tale,
Walking like bride behind the veil.
Jealously I watched them
Carrying golden gems.
The fable of the sea of gold,
With water that adores cold.
Own by the goddess of fortune,
Swam by those opportune,

LOVE AND PARADOX

Tingle my pinna ossicle,
And clutch my ventricle.

Though no water on me smiles,
I kept talking to myself for a long while,
A trial by death no signature stamp.
Little and little with candle and oil lamp,
Labouring night and day with pain,
Some attempt at water treasure gain.

Strides and steps to the seashore,
On sparkling water, I pored.
No gold floats, I knew,
Yet in the sea with icy dew,
The annal is told of whales,
That for food always sail.

My sole by the seaside stood,
Diving is perilous and good,
No lesser than death compared.
Though for this I thus despaired,
Quitting gives mothers and father a failure,
I would rather the pain of death endure.

A million legion of thoughts I sought.
Like a boxer with me I fought.
With the wave roaring my life is at stake.
For some meal the whales seek to make.
Undermining these I dived,
And out I came with a golden fish alive.

LOVE AND PARADOX
Thorns and Fragrance

The beauty of rose is in its fragrance. But beneath this are the thorns. It is a fitting symbol of love: thorns and fragrance.

A thorny rose, so sharp and red.
Its beauty hides the pain ahead,
A symbol of love and passion true,
Her thorns, they could pierce you.

Her fragrance, sweet, and so beguiling,
A bewitching scent that's so alluring.
Its thorns, they guard and keep it safe,
Keeping it from the angelic demon cafe.

A rose so bold, so fierce and free,
Its thorns protect its majesty,
Symbol of strength and courage rare,
A thorny rose, beyond compare.

So tread with care, and do not fear,
The thorny rose, so precious, dear.
For in its petals, love abounds.
And beauty waits to be found,

But held with less care, it wounds.

LOVE AND PARADOX

Broken Tile

The meaning of life is hidden in the scars of its broken rhythm.

When I got home that night
she was asleep in bed in the dark.
I tiptoed here and there and walked
with fear for I didn't want to wake her.
She would cry. Her tears tear my heart.
I didn't want that, so, I didn't bathe.
Bathing is noisy, the rush of shower head,
The splash of waterspout, the brush of
sponge, the banging of bathroom doors.
She would be awake in seconds.
So, I brushed my teeth while the tap
drips with strength three times weaker.
I urinated but didn't flush.
Yet the closing of the lid made her stir.
Come on! How long shall I sneak like a
thief in my own house?
If your sleep rest on your eyelids,
and your slumber sleep by your pinna
and your dreams are just as shallow,

do you want me dead at night
to awake to life in the morning?
When she began to cry, "I want to sleep,
I can't sleep." I said, "I'm sorry."
"No you're not." She said.
And my heart broke like that broken tile
I saw on campus four hours before.
I went to bed but couldn't sleep.
As I lay there, wakefulness walk
through my head.
I turned and moved my head,
insomnia held it still.
Worry overtook me.
Not sleeping is a disease.
I drank a bottle of beer an hour before.
I said, "Beer is evil, it robs one of sleep.
I shall drink it no more."
So, I prayed for sleep as the night wore
away. It passed by and by it went.
My circadian rhythm was broken, like
a broken tile, scarring the pattern,
the intricate form of what should be
my hours of rest woven beneath
the hours of labour.

I accused a bottle of beer, the tiptoeing
of thieves, and the worries of woes.
They broke my night, and my
circadian cycle like a broken tile.

JOSEPH OVWEMUVWOSE

Love and Paradox

Love is the greatest shareholder in the enterprise of human endeavours and it is full of conflicting components.

Love has no definition. It is meaningless in things ugly. It means all things beautiful. Love is tricky. Love is confusing. Love is boundless. Love is bounded. Love is love. Love does things stupid and wise.

Love goes everywhere. Love goes to the park. Love goes to the sea. It goes on pilgrimage. It goes partying. It does not give enough of itself. It gives all of itself.

Love is debilitating. Love is strengthening. Love is a servant. Love is a ruler. Love is a master. Love is a slave. Love is a worshipper. Love is a god. Love is real. Love is a fantasy. Love is a fairy tale. Love is a true story.
Love kills. Love makes alive. Love is a simpleton. Love is a sage. Love is

dangerous. Love is safe. Love is exciting. Love is melancholic. Love is sublime. Love is ephemeral. Love is concrete. Love is abstract.

Love is emotional. Love is rational. Love is irrational. Love is logical. Love hurts. Love heals. Love gives. Love takes. Love smiles and laughs. Love frowns and weeps. Love breaks hearts. Love mends hearts. Love is tears of joy. Love is tears of agony.

Love is fear. Love is courage. Love is cowardice. Love is bravery. Love is simple. Love is complicated. Love is weak. Love is strong. Love is poor. Love is wealthy. Love is health. Love is infirmity.
Love is a tender flower. Love is a hard rock. Love is a rough pebble. Love is a smooth pearl. Love lives in the soul. Love is visible in the body. Love is selfish. Love is selfless. Love is greedy. Love is kind. Love clings to things. Love let things go. Love falls. Love rises.

Love is insane. Love is sober. Love is blind. Love sees all things. Love is the sunrise of the spirit. Love could be the sunset of the soul. Love is dusk. Love is dawn. Love is sadness. Love is joy. Love is a crown of gold. Love is a crown of thorns. Love is the petal and fragrance of rose flowers. Love is the thorn of rose stems and branches.

Love is whole. Love is broken. Love is thin. Love is large. Love is everything. Love is anything. Love is all-encompassing. Love is very exclusive. Love is far. Love is near. Love is there. Love is here. Love is over. Love is ever.

Love could be the delightful flavour of gelato by the sunny beaches of Montpellier. It could also be the acerbic sour savour of an unripe lemon in the salad for dinner.

Love is in the honey from a thousand bees gathered from the honeycomb of apiculturists.

It is also the gull and bitter tang of dark chocolate collected from a minimart by a tourist.

Love is beneath. Love is above. Love is foolish. Love is wise. Love is fair. Love is unclear. Love is cool. Love is weird. Love is hunger. Love is satisfaction. Love needs everything. Love gives everything. Love floats. Love sinks.
Love is the accused. Love is the accusation. Love is a crime.

Love is the prosecutor. Love is the defence. Love is the defendant. Love is the jury. Love is the law. Love is the case. Love is the judge. Love is the verdict.
Love is in everything. Love can leave you with nothing. Love is freedom. Love is bondage. Love is life. Love is death. Love is power. Love is the glory. Love is the purpose. Love is the honour. Love is the essence.

Love is all and all is love. To live is to love. To love is to truly live. Love wears different apparel. The one suitable for an occasion. But in all. Love is eternal. Love is immutable. Love is love. Love is God and God is love.

LOVE AND PARADOX

The Edge of Grief

The lost of a loved one is an experience that pushes one beyond the edge of grief.

I met her few years ago in Lagos,
When we celebrated the fortunes of fate,
She was different in many beautiful ways,
Looking at her move through the crowd.
I called her aunty K, for respect forbids me,
To call her by her name as is our manner.

She wears smooth smiles and kindness always.
Her manner is maturity and love.
Yesterday, I heard she is no more.
Sudden death took her away from me.

Now I'm confused, trying to process it,
I'm walking through the puzzling edge of grief,
Desperately taxing my brain to understand
Why the death-deservings don't always die,
But they who are too alive to die, die early.
So, that is the lot of everyone, right?

That in life we wear mortality like a watch.

I shall miss your smile, concern and care.
I shall miss your wisdom and counsel too.
If I had known that you would go this soon,
I'd have plan for us to meet at least once.

Now you're gone, you took me unaware,
The pain is like grabbing a van of vacuum,
Like reaching for cobwebs in emptiness.
I want to blame someone, something for it.
But I don't know who or what deserve it more.
The death that took you didn't do well at all.
The ailment that ailed you offended me.

This is one of the little things I could do,
To embalm you with the life verses could give,
Constructed in syllables, rhythm, and cadence.
That everyone who reads it might be aware
That you lived a life worthy of immortality.

Dear aunty K,
Your life was well lived, for as much as I know.
I will remember your prayers and care.
I will remember your counsel and concerns.
I will remember your kindness and support.
And I will think about those you left behind.
I won't tell you goodbye, no not now.
By these verses, I'm making you a home,
Among everyone I care about in my heart.

Aunty K, please take care of yourself,
Wherever you're in time and eternity.

JOSEPH OVWEMUVWOSE

Part Three: Society and Politics

At the City Centre
Wine
The Politicians' Pledge
Mad House
The Days of Death
The Dead Head
Neurons and Neutrophils
The Malleability of Modernity
The Ballot and the Bullet
On Strange Tongue
The Twitter Trender
The Mad Maid
The Brand Paradox
The Needy and the Greedy
The Hot Tripod
Rasps of Reeds
I had a Dream
How the World Works.
Boobs and Butts

JOSEPH OVWEMUVWOSE

At the City Centre

What values is there in wandering around city centres, having a bottle of beer, and just sitting lazily around?

While I'm curled up in my bed,
Contemplating how my life is faring,
The whole world is moving on.
I'm just one being among two billion.
No single man can put a full stop
To the progress of history.
Not Putin, or some American.

From my bedroom to the city centre,
I sat on the edge of a fountain,
And watch socialites converse,
Friends with friends, partner with partner.
And I saw a fellow: feminine in front,
But a male from behind,
I have no idea his stage of or no transition.

I see no value in outgoings.
Except to a restaurant for food,
Walking around the city square,

To what purpose is that?
Here they come.
A white and a black guy in plated hair.
Sharing a *rizla* paper to my right,
And another burning flames to my left,
Both are sins that ail my body. I moved.

I am seated at the tram station,
Looking around, watching people,
As they go and come,
I spoke with Ismail,
The Ghanaian mad man,
Tonight, was the the second time,
I had discussed with a black mad French man.
And that was in Paris at first,
His body was scarred and scaly,
He had his last bath a year or two ago.
The madness of one man,
Cannot undo the sanity of all.
Men should know this and learn,
Their place in the course of history.
You came and took your place in time,
And you'll go when your days are spent.

Why not do all the good you can,
To all the people who needs them,
So, when you're no more,
The remembrance of your name,
Shall be a great memorial,
For the children of time.

LOVE AND PARADOX

<u>Wine</u>

Wine is the spirit of civilization.

Here is my bottle of champagne,
That which joyful jubilee contains.
You've poured some into my cocktail.
Its foams narrate our triumphant tales.
He plucked the plug, and it pops
An uproar of the gladness of grapes.
The days of sorrow are gone,
And now is the time for fun.

There they are gathered at the club.
I met some moguls at the city hub.
Their tables are packed with classy tumblers,
That cost a great deal of pounds and dollars.
Fellows, men and women, young and old,
Clothed with expensive silver and gold,
Click glasses, drank their wine that day,
As they chatter and smile away.
I'm bold to say, "Wine is a symbol of wealth,

And of happiness if you have good health.

They call it spirit at times,
This is but a fitting name.
Because wine revive the spirit of men,
Few things cheer men as sharing wine with friends.

Give me a glass, maybe two or three,
When I'm down, a sip could set me free.
They who travels far and wide,
Have tasted of the spirit of other lands,
In their bottles of wines.

The Politician's Pledge

In Nigeria, the politicians who are scoundrels say the national pledge in reverse with their head and heart.

I pledge to Nigeria my country,
To be unfaithful to the people,
But to be faithful to my household,
To be loyal to my pocket and political party,
To be completely and subtly dishonest,
Manipulating the law to favour my quest.

I pledge to Nigeria my country,
To steal from the treasury with all my strength,
To achieve this, I will go all the length,
To buy properties home and abroad,
I'll be a nepotist worshipped as a god,
I'll buy votes and kill to win all elections,
I'll uphold the ethics of defection.
I pledge to Nigeria my country,
To divide the country so I can rule by my tribe,

To be deaf and dumb to the cry of the masses,
To kill with the military and security services,
Everyone that is a dissenting voice,
To reward profanity, impunity, and criminality,
As long as they are in my political party.

I pledge to Nigeria my country,
To denigrate my fatherland with impunity,
And make her lose her honour in the world,
To make all her sons and daughters look like criminals,
So that she will be crown with corruption.
To impoverish her and make her the poorest in the world.

I pledge to Nigeria my country,
To cloth her with shame and rejection everywhere,
To stripe from her every garment of glory,
To cloth her with dishonour all her days.

I pledge to Nigeria my country,
To be a religious fanatic,
To divide the country between religious line,
And to fuel crises based on belief and ideologies,
To pretend to be religious so I can win votes,
And be a hypocrite to win supporters.

I pledge to Nigeria my country,
To inspire my kin to behold the skies above,
As though God alone guides their wealth and dues,
And kill true priests who dare to question and probe.

O God, if you do exist, when life's final breath ensues,
Lay me to rest by priests, a sacred dove,
Or with an Imam's prayer, to worlds anew.
May my gathered spoils feed my family,
But I will ask that you rest my soul in peace.

As I ask for your bosom of my restful repose,
Help me, O God," my plea, I send to you.

LOVE AND PARADOX

Mad House

Politicians everywhere are like mad men. Their greed could turn a decent country into a mad house.

Before the door to the house was broken,
And the peace of the land was taken,
Before he came with a million promises,
And blatantly lied to our faces,

Before we voted for him,
Many turned his name into a hymn.
When he sang the song of the saints,
They believed he would revive the faints.

Before he came from the north,
And connived with those of the south,
Before the bullion vans of the west,
Collaborated with the priests of the east,

Then the land was with good luck,
The farmers their fruits could pluck,
Then we could seat in our homes,
And we could pray in our domes.

Then we were wealthy,
And the economy was healthy,
Then we were free,
And were sure of tomorrow to see.

Alas! Alas!!
Now we are sick,
And tired and falling and dying.

Now ours is a house,
Ruled by the mad and the dead,
Now ours is a madhouse.

The Days of Death

Hope helps us wade through the darkest hours of death.

When I was a child, I was told of a day of doom.
When there would be a chaotic clash between two kingdoms.
One rule by good and the other by the forces of all that is evil.
When the sons of light will destroy all the sons of the devil.
And that that day shall be full of dread and the dead shall be many.
Oh! how my young, terrified heart weighed so sorrowfully heavy.
I closed my innocent eyes and said a prayer, silent but heartfelt.
'Dear God make me a son of light.' I said that while I knelt.
I rose, walked into my day, and forgot the horror of death,
For the story of Armageddon sounds like a myth,

To the head of children who just want to play and enjoy love,
And would not be bothered by adults' dirty gloves.

At least, the days of death were painted in horrendous stories,
Abandoned to the imagination of the mind in all their horrible gory,
That was when I was growing up beside a forest in the Niger.
Where I listened to birds sing and insects chirp over yonder.
I woke up, went about playing, bathed in the river, ate and slept.
My eyes were closed while I dreamt, and the doors were barely locked.
Life was cute, simple, easy and full.
The hands of mothers wiped dirt from the faces and buttocks of playing children, and their soiled shirts.
Fathers came home from the farm, shop and offices to meet their family,

Whole, complete, full, content and hopeful.
None thought of personal fatality.

But now things have changed.
The air wave is poisoned with distress and sorrow.
Every day is now a day of death.
Yesterday it was in the north.
How about tomorrow?

Now I am a man.
My childhood days of innocence are over.
With it went the beauty of peace and that hope of living forever.
Now I know that men do not live eternal in this part of our sphere.
As a sage gone hence many thousand years did say of them going as air,
That men do go to where all men do go to never come is natural.
Just as the corn shall fall on the soil, grow, birth seed and die is normal.
Where it hurts the farmer is when you cut off the stem of his green maize,

While it is in all its prime, with leaves fresh,
luscious and giving the sun a good gaze.
To gather the grains of a grown ground to
the granary of a grower is a great glory.
But to cut off cute crops in cruelty is a curse
to the crooked and the cropper's calorie.
So, it has become of my father land, that
many lives in their primes are being hacked.
While the commander seats in ease issuing
statements for which he should be sacked.

My heart hurts and broken in thirty-six
pieces and one more.
Everywhere, head, hands, legs, belly, feet,
fingers, eyes, and ears are sore.
I am depressed with anguish and sorry has
bought my night and paid for my day,
Everywhere I look in search of an outlet,
there seems to be no way.
I am fed up, and as the sad news keep
shooting up,
I just want to give up.
What shall we do, when on land, water; and
air dead bodies keep piling up?

A damsel, the father's hope was mobbed,
murdered, and burnt in the north.
A man, the mother's dream was mugged,
murdered and decapitated in the south.
Gone are the days when water flowed
across the Benue and Niger rivers.
These are the days when streams of blood
flow, up north, down south and meet at
Lokoja.
I shall be sorrowful and let the tears flow
freely as I pray in hope holding my breath.
While I await that very blissful epoch when
the days of life shall conquer the days of
death.

JOSEPH OVWEMUVWOSE

The Dead Head

That some living men carry a dead head is a strange truth.

The other day the story was told,
Of a man who was sick of a severe cold.
He had all that he needed to be cured,
And did all the pains of the syringe endured.
The best of all physicians watched over him,
And he was checked in all his anatomy.

He got all the treatment money could afford,
And many time he was even flown abroad.
Day in day out he was worse than the day before,
Until the injection points began to break out in sores.
The more they treated him the worse he got.

And the family mustered all courage and fought.
For the sake of love, they would not quit.
To let him die would create a lot of guilt.
Herbalist in red clothes were consulted,
The doctors in white coat they besought.
At times it looks as if he is healthy,
But the odour around him was filthy.

Lying alone in coma on the hospital bed,
He seems he is sleeping from being well fed.
The long black coat wouldn't take his breath,
And he wouldn't dance to the drumbeats of death.
He has become a horrible burden to his family,
And they weren't willing to give him up completely.
Because his chest was still rising and falling,
They kept hoping that he would start talking.
The sibling and the clan have spent all their penny.

And his ailment sent them all into lack and agony.
Parents could no longer afford school fees for kids,
And they began to sell their belongings at very low bids.
His disease has become a social malady,
And soon it will break out into a colossal tragedy.

'Let's leave him and let him die,' says the pragmatic lad.
'You're a fool, who knows nothing, and it's so sad'
Responded an ossified dingbat.
'For when he is up, he will just be as fat'.
So, he laid there, and days turned into weeks.
And with each passing one, he grew weak.
Yet they didn't know that it is so.
On a fateful day, fortune have her way.
A more proficient doctor came to the city,
His heart told him to have some pity.

He walked into the ward and did his examination.
All the contours of his face were exclamations.
With shaking hands, he covered him with the bedspread,
And with enough soothing he said, "His head is dead."

JOSEPH OVWEMUVWOSE

Neurons and Neutrophils

Our brains are told to disagree with what they see as reality. We are told to lie and agree with the feeling of some.

Heart and head,
Brain and lip,
Thought and word.
The menace of fighting forces.
This is what my heart thinks,
That is what my mouth should say.
Magnets works in conflicting poles,
Electricity lives in opposite charges,
The world toils in contrasting ideation.

Can I say what I see and believe to be true,
And walk home safely antagonized?
Can I say a monkey is not a man,
A man is not a woman,
And a woman is not a monkey?
Is there any hierarchy in truth?
Can one truth be truer than another truth?
What if the truth is graded by emotion,
And the colours decide to pale,

So that pink is no longer flushed,
And red decided to be black?
Will the sun still rise from the east,
And travel all the way to the west?
Even though that is a lie,
For the earth floats in space,
While the sun stands by and watch.

Now I declare by the heart and bead of my soul!
That salt is sugar because I feel the same,
Whether I taste one or the other.
Water is urine whether it comes by rain,
Or tap, and all the rivers are full of piss.
And the universe oceans are urinal, unflushed.
Every cooked cuisine in the cooking pot is faeces.
The feacal meal of worms is what you enjoy at dinner.
Every man from London to Lagos feeds on dungs,
The taste of chocolate is a delusion of the taste buds.

I am not a mad man. At least we are sane.
Ours is a world of confusion and deception.
Propagated propaganda, narrative twisted.
Classified truth and publicized lies.
The head and heart, neurons and neutrophils
Disequilibrium, spiteful quarrels.
When the truth is stable,
And what is true is not truer,
The neurons and neutrophils shall agree.
They shall go out and come in,
Respectful of each other.
And the lip shall synchronize with both.

The Malleability of Modernity

Our world has become so malleable that anyone can pretend to mould it into anything he wants.

The pillars of our civilization are crumbling. They're fast becoming piles of gesticulation and pontifical sanctimony made more cynically sinister by a world gone online. Where anonymity and empty emotional gratification are the drives.

The equality of the online world is a knife edge. Good and evil, depending on who wields it. We are falling apart, a dissolved culture. A mixture of confused identities where adolescents and adults clamour for followership in most bizarre undertakings.

Nothing is concrete anymore. There is no sexuality and gender died yesterday. Everything is without boundaries. Whatever is, is what I call it. I'm a man if I so chose. Reality has no say. And or a woman if that's what I want to be. A woman yesterday, a trans man today, and a man tomorrow.

Do not call your newborn baby a boy. Nor should you call the baby a girl. The baby is not a son, the baby is not a daughter. Do not ask me what the baby is because I do not know.

In eighteen years' time, when the ballot is ready for the vote, and the blood had got enough hormones, when the chest becomes flat or bumpy, even then we cannot conclude for sure. For then it shall be by the strength of emotion.

Whether there is a long pole or a very wide hole, this also has no point. Uterus and testicles are biological organs, very submissive to the sharpness of the knife in the hand of an expert surgeon.
"But the father and the mother, how should the pediatrician break the news?" There you

go again. There is no dad or mom. They are parents and that is just enough.

I was told in France of someone who travelled from the home of his parents. He spent a few years away. But when he returned home, the mother whose breasts this traveler suckled had died. She died of transmutation. This traveler was fortunate to now have two fathers or two mothers or two similar parents. Confusing?

And here they come so beautiful and colourful. Proudly riding across the streets in wonderful formation, like the stroke of a master painter. They are strong. They are determined. They have got an army. And they will choke you if you dare say nay to what they say. And many have gown down the drain. Completely canceled.

I was told of an alpha and omega. A man who dwelt many years ago in an abode beyond the mountains of cloud. I heard he was a powerful fellow. But one stronger than he came riding on a polychromatic horse. With the rainbow for a spear and darted him to death. And that was during *The Battle of Equality*.

As it's in all tales, the victor always decides the new order. This was his decision, "I'm the maker of all things reality. There is no science, there are no gods. He, she, and they are no longer sitting in the church pews, not in any shrine or temple or laboratory. They were buried last year in the cemetery. I wore black, did you not see me? I am the god now, the new god of the new age. And my head is the temple, my fingers the shrine and my eyes the microscope. Don't you dare talk about your creator here. I am the god who ever lived and who will ever live."

So, I stand akimbo, amazed, confused? No. I am wondering if this is a delusion of some sort. No, it is financial, political, and psychological. But I am a biologist. I believe in tissues and cells and organs and systems and their interconnectedness.

When will it end? It is an unending tug of war. Yesterday, blouse, today skirt and pants, and tomorrow shoes. Men's feet are bigger than women's, almost, always. Are you sure?

He is a she and her is him, but no they are all they. This is a pot of soup cooked on the fireplace of the malleability of modernity.

JOSEPH OVWEMUVWOSE

The Ballot and the Bullet

Democracy is at times clothed in tyranny and tyranny is most times clothed in democracy.

Elections come and go.
The ballot says so.
But the bullet says no.

Battles come and go.
The bullet says so.
But the ballot says no.

Democracy is the cord of equity.
And it is an enemy of tyranny.
It is meant to glorify honesty.

The ballot gives men power.
The best that could be gotten ever.
Everything works if it's properly delivered.

Ideally, the power of the ballot is for the deserving,

That had been proven by deeds that are satisfying.
Given by all through electoral processes and voting.

Dictatorship is the cord of discord.
The bullet is the sceptre and rod of its lord.
History overflows with its despicable record.

The power of tyranny comes by anarchy,
Through evil and conspiratorial treachery.
It gives nothing but the misery of slavery.

Before us, stands the gentleman, democracy,
And another loathsome scum, autocracy,
Which of these did catch your curiosity?

There is another grief which I'm yet to understand,
Something grievous is going on in my fatherland.

Here, tyranny and democracy go hand in hand.

If the ballot calls the bullet brother during election,
And when the power that be always use intimidation,
Do you think it will be a free and fair competition?

Thinking about this my conclusion is absolute,
Ballots belongs to rare lands governed by elites,
Bullets is for many lands presided over by brutes.

Give us the ballot and democracy,
Destroy every bullet and tyranny,
And may be the world could be happy.

LOVE AND PARADOX

On Strange Tongue

Language has been a weapon of dominion, confusion, and classification. Learn your mother's and learn other tongues.

That very tongue strange to my mother,
A very acerbic alien to the lips of my father,
Caught me in between unpreparedness,
And a hot passion that pursues progress.

Ears healthy but I'm helplessly dumb.
Mouth is virile but my tongue is numb.
I heard everything but I heard nothing.
I composed my thought but said nothing.

The strange tongue,
Made me guilty of a law I didn't break.
It placed my success and future at stake.
The strange tongue robbed me of love,
And like a fool it made men shoved
My mouth as done to men hard of hearing.
And it sure robbed me of a lot of earning.
I tried, I failed, I tried I passed and progressed,

Strange mother's tongues lack short success.
I'm not quitting, strangers could be made friends.
Soon, strange tongue shall be familiar at the end.

LOVE AND PARADOX

The Twitter Trender

Our attachment to social media benefits us less than advertisers.

Twitter *trender*, always in the know.
With every trend, you seem to flow.
But how do you get the time to see?
All the hashtags, scrolling endlessly.

Don't you have a job, a life to lead?
A world beyond the screen, you need to heed.
But you're hooked, it seems, to every tweet,
From dawn till dusk, you never miss a beat.

Marketers target you, with ads galore,
Knowing you'll buy and want even more.
You're their goldmine, their revenue stream,
The Twitter *trender*, the marketer's dream.

Influencers target you, with every post.
Her sponsored content, you love the most.
You buy their products and trust their word.

The Twitter *trender*, a follower of the herd.

Wisdom demands you use your time,
On Twitter, to your benefit, to climb
The ladder of success, with each tweet.
The Twitter *trender*, with a plan to meet.

So use your time, on Twitter, wise
To build your brand, and monetise
Your influence, and your social clout
The Twitter *trender*, without a doubt.

LOVE AND PARADOX

The Mad Maid

The mad maid says sanity is not a necessity for happiness.

Legs stretched in the kiosk,
By a street corner in a house of husk.
Shells of palm nut and coconut,
Among the stench from rubbish rot,
She sings for a dancing swarm of flies.
Till tears touch the teat of pity cries.

Tuft tangled in antiquity and abandoned,
Never touched by caring fingers of one.
Head to feet clothed in plastic dust,
A robe made from a million rag of rust.
Covered skin creamed with dark dry mucus,
The only to her superfluous.

Mulching meal gathered from garbage,
Dumped damp leftover of funeral and marriage.
Drinking mother murderer water,
From a fierce nauseating gutter,
With a calm gulping candour,

And never scared of being a corps.

The air listened to her voice spell,
As to none and all she her tale tell,
Amidst shout in meaningless glee,
For irrationality she has a degree,
Picking and packing plates away,
Arranging them in an ordered disarray.

Queenly dressed in a mini skirt,
In which a thousand cavities flirt,
Face powered in white charcoal.
Is seduction her goal?
Yes, she is the mad maid,
By whom our dudes are raid.

Watching her sing with joy and beauty,
Chanting without a care with such ecstasy,
Sanity is not a necessity for happiness.
Whether glad or sad the mad said to chant in bliss.

The Brand Paradox

Great minds get paid to identify with brands. Little minds pay to identify themselves with brands.

In the realm of western corporation
Where money and all ideas intertwine,
Great minds are paid to align with brands,
To wield their genius their fans to influence
In the pursuit of fortunes their followers fleece,
Where creativity and commerce entwine,
Great minds soar, prosperity they find.

In the realm where thoughts are unrefined,
Little minds seek brands for self to define.
They pay their homage, hearts confined,
For in the labels, they seek their identity,
Following foolishly the foot of strange stars
My feet are branded, my shirt is labelled.
This shirt is a design of the house of Shun.
They forgot that brands are for slaves.
And free and greet men define their apparels.

In marketing's web, a plan devised,
To keep men bound, desires disguised.
Brands entice, illusions prized high,
It is the dance of an enslaved consumer,
A strategy perpetuated to hypnotise,
Enslavement subtle, the fate of fools
Yet knowledge is everywhere,
Yet men fail to seek illumination,
To break free from chains, liberated.

Great souls wear clothes as their own art,
A canvas of expression, a masterpiece's start.
In fabric, they weave their essence's core,
Unfazed by trends, their style they explore.

While small minds cling to outer guise,
Defined by labels, a disguise.
In attire, they seek to belong,
Forgetting within, where strength is strong.
The garments don't make greatness mine,
It's the spirit within, the inner design.
So let us rise above the facade,
And let our true selves be unmarred.

LOVE AND PARADOX

A man's true worth, not cloth adorned,
But the virtues deep, forever sworn.
So let us break the marketing chains,
Reject the grip, where profit reigns.
Freedom from enslavement's maze,
In greatness found, our spirits raise.

JOSEPH OVWEMUVWOSE

The Needy and the Greedy

Politicians in my country are greedy. The masses they represent are in need. What happens when they meet?

The meeting of the needy and greedy
is a clash of discomfort and
a collision of inconveniences.
Like the itching of the ear and
the far abode of the cleaning bud.

Why is one senator worth fifty university professors?
Why is my governor's car costlier than all the teachers?
Why did he use their six months salaries to buy one jeep?

Why should he buy a presidential nomination form?
A former corrupt governor charged for embezzlement,
He has not yet been acquitted of such criminal indictment.

What is it's useful contribution to our national adventure?
The excessive cost of a crook-minded bicameral legislature.
Can't the country do with one; reduce their looting nature.

Why's it costlier than double the annual presidential salary?
The presidential nomination form of a political party.
Is that not a proof of an incentive for public criminality?

Why should I not spit on his face?
When the president is living in a safe place,
He flies our presidential jet wherever he goes,
While captives kidnapped by terrorist are in throes,
Giving birth to his companions' and their rapers' babies,
While imprisoned for lack of ransom in endless captivity.

Why should they demand patriotism from me?
The delinquent gang lords of the wealth of my country.
With what moral authority do they demand my respect,
When their smallest duty to us all they neglect?

Why should they earn the highest salary in the world?
Presiding over the poorest nation of men on earth,
This they do when our common treasury they thirled.
Hurling away our commonwealth, killing my mom's hearth.

He has his children in the best universities,
And those of his cronies in developed countries,
But the president closed the doors of public universities,

With strikes he's swathing our youths and their destinies.
I spit on his face and all those in his administration,
The president in *Asrock* and the governor of my state.
The local government chairman and his associates.
I urinate on their offices and tomorrow shall be defecation.

JOSEPH OVWEMUVWOSE

The Hot Tripod

The alliance of priests and politicians is an evil conspiracy to defraud the people of my country.

In my mother's little thatch roof kitchen,
Made of mud walls, there is an earthen oven.
And besides this oven above the ashes stands a tripod.
Between its legs are the mouths for the dead dry wood.
Above the rings that holds the three legs are three hands,
A big pot of soup of leaves, spices, and meat stands.
Smoke rises from this cauldron as my mother stirred.
I stood at the kitchen entrance and gave mother a stare.
She makes all our meal as the smoke stings her eyes.
My mother must be pained if the hunger here must die.

Tonight, while I contemplate the title of this piece,
To discuss the Aso Rock, Mecca and Jerusalem alliance,
And how much and how many of my people it has fleeced,
The perversion of the umbrella, broom, and the priests,
I was reminded once more of the three-legged tripod,
And how they have deceived us in the name of God.

The imam from Mecca, the priest of Jerusalem,
He is a brother to the father and reverend from Rome.
They meet at Abuja table in the village of Aso rock,
To deliberate how to divide our minds into blocks,
And keep them in chains and locks.
Three legs by which the meal of our country is prepared,

Three legs by which that very meal of oppression is shared.
Three legs that cook the meal of suppression and insanity.
Are two parted into three for two will never agree.

LOVE AND PARADOX

Rasps of Reeds

I'm a proud Nigerian gem, I wear my Africaness like a diadem.

I shall sing the praise
of the heroines and heroes
of my country.
Fellows immortally dead,
Living and gone legends.
Wole gave me a title,
And Chinua taught me riddles.
They advocate,
And their mouths annotate
our stories in pens and saliva dried.
When Chimamanda penned
of families slaughtered
by the gun of the butchers,
we saw the pain of chaos,
in the war of woes.
When men murdered their brothers,
They are sons of second tribal mother.
I shall tell of the days of *Soro Soke*,
When my generation heartily spoke,

And I walked the street of Nottingham,
A city ocean-far from my mother's farm,
With fellow-country youth globe-over,
Singing of a new country order.
Those were the days when our voice,
Aligned with the national choice.
We told them that we matter,
We knew things could be better.

I shall tell of the youth
Of east, west north and south,
Singing the songs of sorrow,
Preaching the hope of tomorrow,
With the Afro beat and flute,
As in the days of Fela Kuti.
When the grey hairs sold their eyes,
The insight of the aged died,
The dark hairs and young teeth,
Decided to crack nuts with faith.
Then we are saying hope,
Even if it is against hope to hope.
This beat has taken the world,
Europe, America, Asia, it swirled.
They dance to the drums of my ancestors,

Who played by the shore of my rivers,
So, I'm a proud Nigerian gem,
I wear my *Africaness* like a diadem.

I shall sing of my hope for progress,
That in the country that is so blessed,
Justice shall kiss love with the law.
And men will heartily confess their flaws,
One to another and resign with honour,
Each becoming a peaceful donor,
When found wanting in public office.

I shall dare to hope for love-sacrifice,
When men shall give up their greed,
That all could meet their very need.
I shall dare to hope that the golden hen,
Which is our country of great men,
Ruined and devastated by the greed,
Of men in power with the rasps of reeds,
Shall once again be revived,
To tell all that the black can thrive.

JOSEPH OVWEMUVWOSE

I had a Dream

I will keep dreaming of the day my country of birth will be worth her salt.

Last night I went to bed tired and quite late,
My day was burden by tasks real and great.
Day's toil had left me worn and frayed,
To the realm of dreams, I gently strayed.

To a land where opulent greens did bloom,
White roses like stars in the green grand room.
Through an unearthly forest, tranquil and still,
Wrapped in nature's equilibrium, a serene thrill.

Angels in delicious dresses, sing songs so sweet,
To their rich and calm mates' drumbeats
Harps strummed by seraphs unseen,
Choruses of hope, a restful dream.

Jubilant cheers from a distance called,
Beyond the bend, where joy enthralled.
Guided by strings of yearning desire,

I tread on the path, my spirit on fire.

I kept walking towards a strange joy,
Which at the string of my heart so draw.
The further I went, the farther I craved to go.
My toes, heart and head, all agreed to do so.

Trees transformed with life's embrace,
Animated guardians, a sacred space.
Welcoming gestures, arms open wide,
As I ventured forth, they are on my side.

A little while, as I walked, a clearing unfolds.
At its centre is a rock from the days of old.
It's *Aso*, with caves of three dozen cubicles.
These are carved by the beaks of an eagle.

Within these are men of my colour and creed,
They are the very definition of the sun's seed.
'We are of the *Naija tribe*', They declared.
'And we are building the Super Eagle Square.'
Naija's tribes, in harmony dwell,

In Super Eagles' Square, a tale to tell.
Men of purpose, colours aglow,
Their dreams aligned, a shared tableau.

Tears, sweat, and blood they'd share,
For prosperity's banner, they'd always bear.
Super Eagle's Castle, stronghold of the heart,
Where *Naija*'s dreams find their vibrant start.

How the World Works

If you want to change your fortune, you must of necessity change your class.

Nothing is perfect. Nothing ever will. The beauty of the most beautiful woman is not the perfection of beauty. There is no perfection in things like beauty. They are qualitative. Qualitative entities cannot be perfect. That's just it. Nothing in the world is perfect, for the world is not perfect.

The world works with categories. Categories of race, class based on social economic status, sociocultural or sociopolitical affiliations. These can be inherited or transferred by gestation.

The world work based on a categorization of power and influence. Men who can wield influence and power, however that is done will surely bear rule over those who cannot. And there is the power of connection and affiliation. This is where religion, secret society, and tribalism dwell. There must be a kind of belonging. You must belong to a category.

There are other characteristics which are essential. One of which is ambition. An absolute determination to survive and thrive no matter what.

The world work on the bases of the understanding of what a moral code is and how to reign over it. Obeying it when necessary and twisting it whenever twisting it will yield a greater benefit to the agent at that point. This is how an imperfect world works.

Boobs and Butts

Everyone is wounded by the objectification of women. It takes away a woman's honour and a man's money.

A question that has bothered me a while,
In the objectification of women,
Your war against and their battle for it,
Videos creators, how do you deal with them?
Entertainment and fashion industries,
Makers of music movies and bikinis,
Who by buttocks and breast, sell films and cloths,
Do you have them in your broad agenda?
Or is their act an art or promiscuity?

Lipa and Lopez, Charlie and Beyoncé,
The teasing of nipples in nude tunes,
In marketing amorous melodies,
They working with costumers and agents,
Give the world tracks in packed stadiums and rooms,
Dancing the dance of stripped seduction,

Like the Ecstasy of their Saint Teresa,
And Aphrodite garb in Greek temples.
Where is the frontier of art and profanity?

For the objectors to objectification,
The fighters in the army of feminism,
The fierce movement of power and blunder
Where do you dine with these nubile videos,
Which the internet brought to my iPhone?
Vixen dancing in lingerie and bare breast,
Placed there for drooling and gullible fellows,
Who find fun in fine flirtatious female.
Is there an intercourse amid fun and iniquity?

Where does your aggressive anger really lie?
Is it with chivalry or with noblemen?
Be mad, yes mad, with makers of movies,
Who by fiddling on what is left of female,
Fork fortune into their fat bank accounts,
Squeezing their juicy butt and bossy boobs,
Impaling them before the cameras,

Like some moist marketing commodities,
Sold on merchants' table at the city square.
The feminine body's honour, where's it?

Nothing sells like nice titillating teats,
Hidden behind netted and translucent dress.
Leggy models, clad in lewd threads and strings,
Sits on sofa, smiles, selling seats and tables.
Why is that hot blond with the cold freezer?
What are the mechanics of a brunette
On the engineering of a car engine?
What has my short pack of cereal to do,
With the long leg of a thin smiling blonde?
Do you sell your own honour and utility,
At the market of impropriety and nudity?

They conspire to exploit me of my earnings,
Advertisers and models are partners.
The seductive smiles of a stripped ebony,
Plotted with the mulato's spanners and screws,
In the nude valley of excited emotions,

Twisting my hormones, sucking my money.

The war against the objectification,
Of the feminine form in all its forms,
Can only be won when women all over,
Unite against theirs and our exploitation.
They take your body; they take my money.
We are victims of their conspiracy,
Marketers, models, music-movie makers.

LOVE AND PARADOX

Part Four: Religion and Philosophy

The Sermonizing of Semen
Let us Prey
The God Maker
The Fortunes of Fiction
The Manipulation of Man
The Deadly Tome
The Death of the Dead
Foes and Friends

LOVE AND PARADOX

The Sermonizing of Semen

In my country everyone is sermonized from the sperm to the grey hair and the grave.

That fateful night of copulation,
When he was doing the deed of procreation,
That usually precede the period of fertilisation,
A sermon was buzzing from the church next door.
And when the semen flowed to where it should,
At the point of that exhaustive climatic pleasure,
There was a shout, 'Your seeds shall fill the earth,
As the water covered the sea.'
And he said, 'Amen.'

In eight months and one,
The other one with whom he did the deed,
Was big and full of two lives.

In all the days between the night of copulation,
And that joyful painful day of gestation,
There were sermons, sermons, and sermons.
Homiletics on the altar, lecterns, and pulpits.
Exhortation at the dining table and buses,
Tracts on the road and streets.

From the day of the copulation,
And in the hours of his fertilisation,
He had been harangued by heaven's vicars.
Representatives of divine things from above.
He ate creeds of the ancients for breakfast,
And daily wine of blood for the divine dinner.
He was raised to be of the spirit,
Walking by the laws of the realms above,
Among men who lives below.
The day he swam in the semen,
As a half man in search of his second half,
He met her at the bloody gate of the uterus,

In darkness the two halves collided,
And nucleus fused with nucleus.
They became one cell,
While their sources are saying amen,
To a sermon from a shrine next door.

So, from that tropical land of the black,
He was conceived on the lips of sermon,
He lives, moves, and have his being in homiletics,
He is conscious of the afterlife,
His consciousness of the present life
Is coloured by how he thinks of the invisible.
And as he cast his gaze above,
Everything below is in disarray.

This is what befall them,
Who dwell in the land,
Where men are sermonized
from the semen to the grave.
How useful is the sermonizing
Of the semen to our civilization?

JOSEPH OVWEMUVWOSE

Let us Prey

While the masses are praying for the wellbeing of their leaders, these leaders are plotting to prey on them.

While we're praying for their success,
They're preying on our progress.
While we're praying for our progress,
They're preying on our resources.
And they want us to close our eyes,
As men often do in times of prayers.

We are their prayer warriors,
They are our predators.
The priests know all about it.
When we stand on our feet,
When we go down on our knees,
As in the supplication of the Holy See,
They are killing us with their toes,
Like men often do to their foes.

While the worshippers are gathered,
Chanting praises on holy weekends,
Heeding homiletics and exhortation,

LOVE AND PARADOX

And lifting sanctified supplication,
To holy heaven in prayer
For the wellbeing of leaders,
These leaders are plotting to prey
on them even as they pray.
This is happening in Aso Rock.
What a paradox!
To pray!
And to be preys!

JOSEPH OVWEMUVWOSE

The God Maker

Men makes gods who makes men who makes gods who makes men ...

In Greek men creates gods.
In Africa men creates gods.
In Asia men creates gods.

Men fashion gods, and gods mould men,
A timeless cycle, again and again.
Through history's course, this truth transcends,
From ancient days to modern trends,
Divinity, we seek, and then,
Our reflections in gods, we comprehend.

In Greece, gods forged from mythic lore,
Their legends spread from shore to shore.
Olympian heights they did explore,
In tales of triumph, love, and war,
Inspiring mortals to adore,
Their wisdom sought forevermore.

In Africa's lands, gods' spirits rise,

LOVE AND PARADOX

Connecting souls beneath vast skies.
Ancestral whispers, echoes wise,
Guiding hearts as time flies,
In nature's rhythms, spirits comprise,
The essence of life, where hope lies.

In Asia's realms, divine tales unfold,
Where faith and culture interwove.
From mountaintops to rivers' hold,
In temples grand, beliefs enfold,
Celestial wonders they behold,
In reverence, the mysteries untold.

Men's creations, gods abound,
In every corner, beliefs resound.
Yet in our quest, may it be found,
A unity of souls unbound,
Beyond the idols' earthly mound,
To love, compassion, and peace profound.

God and the first man,
Who made who?
I am not talking of the Adam.
Nor am I speaking of reptile ancestor.

When the first man came to know,
That his left hand is not a leg,
Nor his eye an ear,
When did he know that there is a god?
Did he make the god or did god make him?
My father did import a god once.
He kept him is his room.

LOVE AND PARADOX

The Fortunes of Fiction

Writers of fiction can make and kill men. They can make and kill gods. They can impoverish and enrich nations.

First of the blessedness of fiction,
Is the liberty it avails the writer.
It is a very necessary refuge of escape,
For some whose mind dwells on the ideal.

The world is a convoluted place.
By writing fiction I can set it plain.
I can arrest criminals and charge them.
I can create the court, the jury,
The prosecutor and the defendant.
I can also make the judge.

In my fiction I create the constitution.
And I give the judgement.
This is how I write.

It is very simple here,
If you commit the crime,
You must do the time,

The bad guys go to jail.
And if the offence I made him commit,
And of which I convict him,
Is punishable by death,
I ask the hangman to do his job.

The blessedness of fiction,
Is that it provides me an escape
from the madness of the world.
When the president wrongs me
in the hours that I'm awake,
I walk home into my room
and make him ask for mercy
for his wrong on his knee
in ink and paper
and the key of the keyboard.
I accept his apology and forgive.

When Chinua Achebe killed Obinka,
and walked the ways of the gods,
in the Arrow of God,
I'm wondering and happy.
By making gods and threatening
to kill them he tells me the enormity

of the power of the pen.

For writers are fittingly call authors,
for in writing, they wield authority,
that could make them kill or make alive.
They make and kill gods and men.
She decides their time and destiny.
He creates and destroy cities and universes.
And I'm asking, "Between god
and the author, who is mightier?"
My answer is this,
"God makes authors and authors makes gods."
It is left for you to decide the nature of the deity.
And to write is to be elevated and elevates.

JOSEPH OVWEMUVWOSE

The Manipulation of Man

Religious texts are some of the most potent weapons by which men are manipulated.

What if by the interpretation of divine text,
Listener's hands are weakened by pretext,
So that by casting their desire above,
They fail to attend to things beneath,
And that by the passage of time,
The people be made so poor and inutile,
Their mind barren and their hand bare,
They become the object of use,
By they who have taught them so.

What if, in sacred texts, meanings intertwine,
Yet hands of listeners, lost in design,
Bound by pretext, truths they can't divine,
Their focus soars, while roots decline,
In mystic verses, wisdom lies,
But grasping higher, they despise,
Neglecting depths beneath the skies?
A tragic tale, the heart complies.
In casting yearning above the ground,

LOVE AND PARADOX

Neglecting treasures, silently abound,
The world below, unseen, unfound,
In heavens' grasp, but earth's not crowned.
Ephemeral dreams, they chase with zest,
Yet soil neglected, life's true test,
Blinded eyes, they can't attest,
To hidden gems that lie in rest.

As time's relentless river flows,
The plight of people, the sorrow grows,
Poverty's grip, like thorns it sows,
Inutile minds, trapped in throes.
Once vibrant souls, with dreams to hold,
Now shackled, drained, and uncontrolled,
Their spirits weep, their worth untold,
Manipulated, their fate foretold.

Their fertile minds, once vibrant and rare,
Now lie barren, a desolate affair,
Stripped of knowledge, they stand bare,
Pawns in the game, unaware.
Tools of use, their purpose marred,
By those who played a twisted card,
In shadows cast, their souls jarred,

The manipulation, life's facade.

Many a times, preachers in pretext
Take the text out of context.
In order to con men.

LOVE AND PARADOX

The Deadly Tome

Books can kill or make alive. Their power of life and death is much more potent when they are supposedly inspired.

Many years before my conception,
Beside a forest in the Niger Delta,
My fatherland was invaded.
By men bearing arrows, bows,
Bullets, spears, and guns.
And another weapon, fierce,
Vicious, a harbinger of death.
It's subtly weak yet vile in foolish fury,
Burning in unguided wrath.
Its rage is brutal, led by madness,
Wrapped in a leather bag of deception.
Its bearers came through the north dry desert.
They are the emissary of the man of Medinna.

They brought the book of death.
In their hand a tool of fatality.
Death to reason.

Death to knowledge.
Death to peace.
Death to liberty.
Death to civil disagreement.
The demise of everything freedom.
With the guns, arrows, and bows.
They subdue the people.
With the book,
They subjugate them in perpetuity.
With the book,
They made slaves of men.
With the book,
They turn them to vultures of hell.
With the book,
They enslave their mind.
The book makes religion,
A religion bathed in fatal savagery.

The years crept by,
My land was polarized,
Caught in ideological polemics,
That births eternal conflicts,
 That kill and cause mournful sighs.

God is invisible not to the theologians,
Bearing the northern book.
His dead prophet yet speaks,
Speak against him, you are dead.
Dead by a mob.
A mob mobilized by madness,
And manipulation of the mind.
God is omnipresent.
No! He is not there!
He lives in Sokoto right here!

Ours is a faith of peace and love,
To kill an unbeliever is our duty of care.
That is what Ah-leetaf,
 The gentlest, commanded us.
I'm labouring for paradise reward,
Can't you see?
I can marry a girl child of nine,
Like Manismad and Aisha.
And if I kill enough,
In the world to come,
I could live forever,
With seven virgins.
To us down north,

JOSEPH OVWEMUVWOSE

Women are half-of-men,
We lock them in closets.
These are the pillars,
That hold our faith.
The lessons we learned,
From seventh-century Arabia.
We give and take life,
 As the prophet's commands.
Obeying him, our divine destiny.

That book is the book of death. And it's that book that kills Nigeria. When an innocent Nigerian girl is murdered and her body sets ablaze in cold blood just for having an opinion different from the book's while Nigeria looks on in apathy Nigeria dies. The book kills her.

This sad story of the aged tome,
Was passed to us from our fathers.
There is an evil news,
The landlord of Asso is addicted,
He burns this book,

Drinks its dissolved dregs in tea.
He sniffs it as tobacco.
It permeates his brain,
It flows in his vein.
He is addicted to it.
His colleagues, cabals,
Brothers, friends, families,
And they all, incorrigible addicts.

Their policies and politics,
Are those of fanatics.
Blinded to all but the dead man,
To him they are devoted.
Though dead he yet speaks to them.
He tells them to pardon governors,
Whose thievery is killing thousands,
And sinking the ship of the nation.
He tells them to take the lives,
Of those who merely dissent.
The book has wasted Asso's landlord,
It inebriated his judgment.
This is where it has brought us,
A country at a cataclysmic collapse verge.
It enslaved the northern mind,

And subjugates intellect, the book.
And turns men into venomous brutes,
And cold-blooded murderers.
It tells Asso 's landlord thieves to acquit,
An innocent dissent child to murder.
It teaches their emirs to steal.
It teaches hypocrisy and inequity.
It bears repression, division and death in its pages.
It teaches young men to be stupid and unruly.
It gives them the mechanism of murder.
That book is the very book of death.
It's that book that kills Nigeria.
For when an innocent girl is murdered in cold blood for having an opinion different from the book's while Nigeria looks on in apathy, Nigeria dies. The book kills her.

LOVE AND PARADOX

The Death of the Dead

Some men are alive but dead while others who have died are yet alive.

Tonight, rest escaped my eyelids,
While I rehearsed the dance of the dead,
As we usually do every night and day.
Though this is scary you may say,
But really, to sleep is to die.
Sleep and death share a close tie.
This should have given us insight,
That we should not from death take flight,
Because he who has gone to sleep,
Has tasted what it means to fall asleep.

It seems I have gone astray,
Actually, I didn't miss my way.
I was trying to create a synonym,
To usher in the explanation of my theme.

When he said,
"Let the dead bury their dead",
I told myself to take heed.

There he was pointing at two lifeless men,
For lifeless men to bury others is an omen.
But the speaker is not a product of semen,
This is why believing it, I had.
Even though it is hard,
And terribly sad.

The death of the dead man!
But how can a dead man die?
Before you give my poem a ban,
And walk away with slighting sigh,
Give me some time to explain.
Perhaps we can some wisdom gain.
And you won't read it in vain.

There are dead men walking our streets,
And I'm not talking of zombies and ghosts.
These are men healthy with flesh and blood.
Only that their ways are with good at odd.
I heard their hearts passed away,
From the news by what they did yesterday,
It was during a psychic surgery,
Masterminded by the knife of apathy,

Drawn through the aorta in the heart,
And shred all its veins and arteries to tiny parts.

And so, they can never ever give love,
As commanded from above.
And this is worse than a painful sore.
These are our woes since the days of yore.
When a man loses his ability to be good,
He is not better than the bacteria's food.

The other day,
I overheard some people pray,
"God please kill him."
When it became a hymn,
For people to rejoice at your funeral,
Then your living makes life fatal.
And a curse added to the woes of mortals,
If your epitaph is devoid of grievous weeping,
Then your living was worse than dying.
When a man loses his conscience,
This is his first exit from sentience.
When a man dies with his conscience alive,

He is forever never dead.
There are men who die twice,
There are those who never die.
They of the death of the dead man rave,
When his conscience precedes him to the grave.

LOVE AND PARADOX

Foes and Friends

Light and darkness, friends and foes. Such is life. Good and evil are the lots of man.

May the gods urinate on your altars.
May angels' wings be broken at your table.
May all the demons feast on your intestines.
May heaven become hell.
And let paradise wear darkness for a royal apparel,
May the gods of death die the death of men.
May the judgement of the gods be swift and certain.
May men judge the gods,
May men condemn the gods to hades.

Let light and darkness mingle.
Let the sun and the rain conspire against you.
May the ground of the earth and the cloud of the sky,
Celebrate your downfall.

May the winds of the day and spirits of the night,
Unite in your pursuit.
May the birds of the forests and the firmament,
Sing a dirge for you.
May the dawn of day bring you distress.
May the water of the sea,
And the salt of the ocean,
Writes you an awful epitaph.

May the gods sprinkle fragrance on your altar.
May angels' wings be strengthen above your bed.
May demons and pains be far from your entrails.
May all your torments be transformed to paradise.
May your bliss wear radiating royal attires.
May your mortal life take on the divine life.
May your vindication be swift and certain.
Judge not so you won't be judged.
And may you be acquitted in all inquests.

May the light of your life not be tainted by darkness.
May the sun and rain unit in your favour.
May the ground of the earth below,
And the cloud of the sky above,
Connive to celebrate your elevation.
May the airstream of the day,
And the spirits of the night,
Unite to hasting your progress.
May the birds of the forest and the firmament,
Sing you a melodious tune.

May the dawn of the day bring you excitement,
May the rising of the sun bring you sweet songs.
May the setting of the sun bring you rest and peace.
May the water of the sea,
And the salt of the ocean,
Writes you an adorable epitaph.

JOSEPH OVWEMUVWOSE

Part Five: Race and Diversity

The Black Man's Nod
Black and Whitening
Bents and Straights
Black and White
Dusk and Dawn
Oceans and Deserts
Me and My Hair
Ajekpako and *Ajebota*
Wild White West
Compressive Ambivalence

JOSEPH OVWEMUVWOSE

The Black Man's Nod

The black men's nod is much more than a silent salutation.

Each time they see me,
> By the nodding of their heads,
>> They sum up our tales.

LOVE AND PARADOX
Black and Whitening

Blacks have bought the lies that they are not good enough in many ways and as such they are whitening themselves.

When Fela Kuti chanted of Yellow Fever,
And sits it on the delicious Afro beat,
I know he is talking to my heart of black.
When the ladies and gentlemen wear,
The hide of chalk by stripping themselves,
Of their clothes of womb and umbilical cords,
Which married the snow in the feast of melanin,
They become multicoloured in fingers and toes.

I sat in front of the television and watched
the newscaster moved the strange hair,
from her forehead, and earlobe and eye,
'That's not yours,' I said to her, very amused.
In all ways she is a fool, who shed her hair
to wear another's very foreign and strange.

Do to the hair whatever you might,
So long as it is yours and yours alone.
Then you're sitting on the mighty throne
of your true, real and only royal self.

In the West, it is easier to be a Will Smith
than to be an Ovwemuvwose.
Even the computers are conjured alike,
to tell my name and place of birth apart.

Blacks break free from the chains of lies,
Hugging strength that never dies,
No more whitening, no futile tries.
In melanin's pride, our spirit flies.

When to Fela Kuti's songs we dance,
The lineal steps to the Afro beat,
Let this be the echoes of our pride,
Let our hearts dance to the rhythm,
Of our ancestral spirits.
In colours bold, we stand as one,
Embracing our hue under the sun.
Our beauty shines, from the tropical glare,
Authentic selves, we've to keep by name.

Let this song ring far and wide,
To the beautiful ladies of Africa.
Cast away those strange crowns,
And wear each strand your very own,
The heritage of your paternal blood.

Be true to your melanin, name and hair.
Let the masks fall, and let you face be bare,
To your destiny be a master real and brave,

That we are all headed for the grave,
Shows that all men are the same.
Whether they be men of fortune or fame,
Or men of obscure or very few means.
So, embrace your roots, your sacred source,
Unveil the essence, stay the course.
In being you, reclaim your identity.
Let truth and pride be your amenities.

JOSEPH OVWEMUVWOSE

Bents and Straights

Freedom of speech is a fundamental human right.

I'm full of words.
My psychological entrails,
are about to spill.
It will be an outburst.
Being victimized ones for words
uttered, an invisible cork has been
knocked into my gob.
Now I fear words more than death.

But is this not an affliction?
It's a biased justification of their right,
And the denials of that that is ours.
When the horizon is painted with the rainbow,
Should that stop the wind from its journey?
Or that the day is bright,
Should there be no night?
I'm vexed with pains.
It's not for hatred,
But of deprivation.

LOVE AND PARADOX

That I cannot say
What I have to say.

How long shall we murder bio-systems?
Should they die because psychology say so?
And if hormones must go through syringe,
For the voice to become deep,
Is that not insinuating,
That when we turn the cone
Upside down on its tip,
We need to support it to stand?
Why not let it stand on its base?

I am all for love.
And I shall not preach hate,
Neither will I revere what is wrong.
Everything is not black,
Nor is everything white.
But if a forty year old man
Calls snow black,
Am I not permitted to say
He is colour blind?
Your belief is yours.
My belief is mine.

What about the truth?
Do we have that luxury,
To make subjective, actuality?
If you're of the family of the relativists,
Can you argue against the force of gravity?
Can you also say,
I have more or less than two legs?
Can you deny what is in between them?

Have your say.
But don't kill my voice.
I'm all for love.
But if I see what is wrong,
By the ethics that I uphold,
Don't snuff my suffrage,
If I say it is erroneous.

For in that you are an oppressor,
A killer of the liberty of men.
So, let the straights have their say,
As the bents are having their ways.

Black and White

I am who I am, deal with it.

Racism is a menace.
So is discrimination of any form.

Black and white are the two extremes,
Betwixt are Asians, mixed and other themes.
He that is a racist to me is an idiot,
Tied to his umbilical cord by two strings.
One of the misdeeds of his wicked ancestors,
And two, his infantile and biased foetal inclinations.

When I'm treated with discrimination,
By a fellow from another nation,
Because of my race and skin colour,
I enjoy a period of a sad smile with honour.
Smile because I'm having fun at his foolishness,

And sad because I'm saddened by his denseness.
He is a fool not to know that melanin is just skin deep.
He should have learnt, being tanned by the summer sun.

To you I'm not inferior.
To you I'm not superior.
You're my equal,
Based on the content of the cell.
If you shall but say,
"That some animals are more equal than others."
You're an Orwellian animal,
Fit for an animal farm,
And a misfit in the society of humans.

Those who discriminate,
Those whose stigmatize,
Based on sexual orientation,
And gender and disability,
And racial backgrounds,
And socioeconomic status,

Either have a decaying brain,
Or a skull smaller than a sand grain.
He is a crackpot, who refuse to grow
Out of his immature past, into the
Present of knowledge, equity and freedom.
Such is he who claim superiority,
By his self-devised parameters.

JOSEPH OVWEMUVWOSE

Dusk and Dawn

White light is a rainbow at peace with itself.
The cause of division is the wedge of a prism.

As my black ink dance on this white paper of my writing pad. Marked with parallel grey lines to guide my hands from erring. The sun is no more. Here in the South of France, it went to bed sometime after dusk.
Behind my window stand some simple pine trees, beautiful in the day. Invisible in the night. The dead and drying needle-like leaves are not yellow and brown anymore. They are coal black. Yes, the wooden cones. Are not brown anymore, they are as black as pitch.
The ashen speckled bark is no more wooden brown, it is a sable. Even the blossoming roses of red and white buds are no more. They are ebony. The yellow painting of my wall is gone, it is a night.

Oh! how I earnestly wait for dawn.

When the wealth of nature shall be revealed.
In the beauty of all their shades in diversity.

And this diversity is an alluring wonderful story of the abundant riches of this blue dot in space. The variety of paintings created by the stroke of its brush, the glorious plumes of the peacock, the marvels of that calm chameleon, and the powerful patterns of the monarch butterfly's wing. How about the gloriously adorned rainforest of the sea of coral reefs of manifold pigmentation? A living rainbow beneath the ocean obeying the physical laws of chaotic order.

From the grandeur of the Amazonian rainforest; mushrooms, insects, flowers, leaves, and light mingling in a radiant bliss, creating an equanimity that pulls at your heart, To the lily of the valley of our grandmother's garden smiling with its white

teeth besides its hibiscus neighbour waving back with its purple bloom.
They in their harmony revel in their diversity and continually proclaim,
"To be alive is to harmoniously flourish with fluorescence".

My mother heard this and she got herself a mortar and water. And so made some dyes and got my shirt sprinkled. Your shoe is black and brown because the dye said so. Your uncle's white car coating is a sibling of your neighbour's pink blouse. The red blood in my vein had once mixed with the achromatic tears on that baby's cheek. The black hair on my scalp holds hands with the pupils of his blue eyes.

Things living and inanimate, things mighty and minor, participate in this connective narrative of colours. And they also tell the story of change. The change of a progressive kind.

And here I come in this story of shades. That, that red tomato was once green. That juicy lemon was once verdant. Colours are reminders of the permanence of change. That things give way for others. Like tones, what is may no longer be. Life, like colours, does fade.

My hair is black, hers is blond. And maybe yours is brown. But with the passage of time, all these will give way to grey. Tinctures tell the tales of our lives. And the multiplicity of animate nature always comes to unity in humus: dark-black-grey. Buds of divergent hues, furs, and hairs of diverse pigmentation, agree on one thing: a greyish decay.

Dawn is fast approaching. Darkness shall give way to light. Natural radiance so pure and single and yet it is the union of seven friendly fellows. If today is not cloudy, then I shall not see the rainbow. Because it shall be quiet, for white light is a rainbow at peace with itself. Diverse and sundry but single and whole.

Like the conversion of acid in the womb of citrus from that acerbic anger to a sweet refreshing lemonade. In the process of ripening so do I hope for the evolution of humanity. When his vision of colour shall come to maturity.
At that time all the seven colours shall come to a state of equipoise. In which red shall be in total harmony with the indigo. When men of all races, faces, and creeds shall embrace an imperfect symmetry. In which they would be united in their distinctness.

Then the prism of division would have been taken away. And the spectrum would come into an agreement with itself. And the rainbow has metamorphosed into the white light.

It shall be our constant reminder that; we will become as whole as white light when our diversities find their point of equilibrium. And that shall be the dawn of a new beginning.

Oceans and Deserts

The illegal migration issue in the world is two-sided. It is a necessary inconvenience masterminded and caused by various interests.

Until death calls, life will not respond. Life answers to itself through hope. It pushes in search of a higher state to attain and sustain that which gladdens. There is that mysterious state which the finger must relinquish if it will guard its mad sanity. He who has reached will continue to reach some more. It is an illusion that deludes all. Here is a tale I was told of a fine fellow who was caught up in this affable affair of frolicking.

A fellow sired by a father of fat fortune and a mother of modest moods. He grew up in all the goods his nation affords by association but not by merit. The relations that serve the good of a few and the ill of the lots. The camaraderie of common class and interest - to oppress, suppress and deprive the outsiders. But fate frowns at filth, although not frequent enough, and crocked foundations crack with age. And friends could turn foes, so brother, be true to your heart and your heart alone.

His father's friends betrayed him to death and to his father's estate he is no longer an heir. The chief justice gave it to the state governor by the law of the land and his mother died of a heart attack. Those which made him fat have made him lean. His life has shattered to shreds and his future a starless night.

An orphan, thrown to the street, hopeless and miserable. A child abandoned by fate, frustrated by his country norms, and disappointed by the world. At least, death has not named him yet. He would have to answer to himself by hope. He would seek that state of satiation, where all things will be flawless. But that place is as evasive as water in a sieve. Elusive! But we pursue still. The pursuit of happiness is the golden cord of life. The hope of its attainment is the knot of survival. To hope is to live.

He met a friend on the street and that friend took him to another friend. And that another friend took him to another of his friends. He met friends on a third-degree level finally. His first-degree friend walks on foot and he goes through deserts. His second-degree friend walks on water and swims through oceans. His third-degree friend is skin-deep different from their kinds and walks on air. And he is from across the Mediterranean.

And those were a dozen years of orphanhood. The street had made him into a fine fellow. Dexterous and brutal in the ways of the hood. Sly in disposition and lean in love. The school of the street is the college of the jungle. The modules are primitive grit, mischief, and loyalty by interest. He is good at these and many more and they say, he is a good man. And then he crossed his territory and sin against a rival. The unforgivable sin of the street. He would have to atone for this by his blood. To stay is to perish, and to run is to survive.

He turned to his friend from the Sahara route and that spoke to his second-degree friend from Ville de Calais. His second-degree friend spoke to his third-degree friend in the city of Dover. And his first-degree friend from the Sahara gave him this admonition.

"You shall go by the night hours when most men are fast asleep. Ours is a business of the dark. But before the journey you shall with this broom swear, while you are covered with an umbrella. That you shall pay me my fair share. Your umbilical cord shall remain in a calabash beyond the forest of the ancient. The journey shall be perilous I must warn. You shall sleep with scorpions and ride on serpents. You shall sleep in the frost and biting cold of the night and wake by the dusty wind and scorching sun by the day. You shall be thirsty to death and for life, you shall drink your urine. If by chance you die, other pilgrims shall feed on your carcass as bread for breakfast, and brunch and dinner. That is the way of the desert.

If by and by you fail to die, there is a life of the bleached beyond the sea. The Sahara shall bid you farewell, and the Mediterranean shall bid you welcome. And the oceans and seas shall say, "These are the illegal immigrants of the global south – Africans, Asians, and poor Europeans. You are welcome to the hope of all the despairing of the world. Ours is a heavenly country on earth, where all things are fair, beautiful, and just.""

He stepped on the dinghy and paddled in the peril of the sea. The waves rose and fell. Dehydration and death pierced his very marrow. Thirsty while sitting on the ocean of water, the liquified desert. The wave swallowed twelve of his fellow pilgrims and vomited their bloated cadaver on the beach of Calais four days later. Two others disappeared, lost forever. Children and youth full of life and hope. He survived on the *Deo Barents* of the saviour of the west, but stressed and traumatized.

They came with camera and media crews, to make videos of their charity and heroism and the dejection of the migrants and to count them as numbers. The data, keep mounting. They shall be processed like goods and kept in squalors like unwanted commodities. And tonight, it shall be announced on BBC, Aljazeera and CNN and written as a front-page all over the newspapers of the world. "More than five thousand migrants were rescued while crossing the Mediterranean to seek asylum in Europe and more than fourteen of them could not make it." They will feel good about their heroism. They are making the world a better place.

Someone was tempted to tell them otherwise. Because the hypocritical saviours are the creator of the conditions of illegal migration. You are the makers of modern slaves and servants. They are illegal immigrants. They are employed in your companies to labour night and day for meagre wages while you drink and sleep and party. And you romanticize the governor who took his father's estate from him and you call him your ally from the south. You want stability that deprives them of their humanity but powers your pocket. You are the maker of monsters.

And here he comes, scrubbing your floors, cleaning your toilets, and packing your plates. He lifts the heaviest load and does the meanest job and lives in the most deprived condition of the city. He is an immigrant. He pays his taxes but gets no benefit. He is unqualified.

And you say you want to stop illegal immigration? Why will a man terminate a business that gives him profits and helps him feel good among his peers? Please do not answer. The fault is not entirely yours. His country is a place where the masses have no mass. They do not exist. So, you can do to them as you please because they have gone through oceans and deserts to escape the perils of inhumanity.

JOSEPH OVWEMUVWOSE

Me and My Hair

My hair is much more than a mane. It is the summary of my story and the emblem of my identity.

Hair, oh hair, a crown from my territory.
A canvas for the expression of my story.
A symbol of heritage and pride,
A reflection of my ancestral tribe.
Black and dark, short and wild,
Thick and curly, or neatly styled,

A texture and hue unique to my type,
A beauty that shines through, no hype.
It frames my face and shapes my look.
A simple touch can transform a nook.
A flick, a twist, a brush, a braid,
A world of styles that can be made.

But my hair is more than just a mane.
It carries the memories, joy, and pain,
It tells a tale of my life's journey,
A marker of time, symbol of my identity.
So let your hair be what it may,

LOVE AND PARADOX

And wear it proud, day by day,
For in its strands, you'll always find,
A beauty that's truly one of a kind.

JOSEPH OVWEMUVWOSE

Ajekpako **and** *Ajebota*

I have come a long way and I have a long way to go.

This is the tale of my childhood,
The words of my teenage years.
That characterize my journey,
From forest homestead of the Niger Delta,
To the beautiful museums of Europe.
When else you look at my curly hair,
And my chocolate coated skin,
Do remember I'm a child of the sun,
And my journey has been a long one.

The journey of the *Ajekpakos* of the world,
Who must clear their own paths,
Birthed into a family of a hundred siblings,
Among nephews older than their uncles,
To a father too old to count a tuft of a black hair,
To an African mother of seven children.
While you look at my black pupils
With those blue *Ajebota*'s eyes of yours,

Remember that my journey has been long.

I am an *Ajekpako* beloved of my mother,
Hated by my president, forsaken by my governor.
I bought my school desk from my poor pocket,
And other paraphernalia I needed to study.
Read all nights by the faint light of a wick,
Of a weak and dying flame of a tiny cylindrical candle,
Wrestling with mosquitoes.
I defied the odds of poverty,
And triumphed over want's gravity.

While I bathe in an *Ajebota*'s river,
Don't judge me by my complexion.
That fortune has smiled on you,
And apportioned you a place,
By the land of the setting sun,
You have no right to bear me cruelty,
For my journey has been a long one.

I came over deserts,

Swam across seas,
Climb mountains,
Conquered weathers,
Arrived *Ajebota*'s gate,
If I can't find the key,
I shall burst it open.

LOVE AND PARADOX

Wild White West

The wild white west is just another abode of human on earth.

From the days of my umbilical cord,
To the day I saw my first beard strand,
The west as the way has been the standard,
The plumb line of things straight and right.
The walking and living conscience of humanity.
This belief was firm in my virgin heart,
Unsoiled by the benefit of books and movies.
Now I'm sitting staring at the screen,
There are thousand and one documentaries,
In addition to books authored by the victims of the west's cruelty,
Telling me that the wild white west,
Is just like any other part of the world.

I came and sat on the seats of the west,
In paths untraveled, secrets lie discreet.
By the favours of fortune and fate,

I journeyed from the tomb of my umbilical cord,
Across the oceans of water on the air highway.

Then I tasted the cruelty of the west.
The police for me a suspect took,
Just because my melanin shouted at him.
A youth hit my head with an empty can,
Just because my hair is not as straight as his.
Then I know it is the wild white west,
Another habitat of men in the world.

And I slept, and dreamt and hoped,
That my childhood view shall me restored,
That in the west, the air bubble of the plumb,
Shall always be at the centre of the liquid medium,
That the compass will always point to the north,
That the sun will always rise from the east,

That the truth will always oppose falsehood,
That square pegs will never be placed in round holes,
That smiles will genuinely express heartfelt kindness,

Alas, I was disappointed, my dreams died discontented.
And I remembered that I'm not in heaven, but in the white wild west.

The wild white west is another abode of human,
Made of flesh, bone, and blood.
Angels live in heaven, humans live on earth.
In earth's arm, the wild white west abides.
Men lie, cheat and murder in the wild white west.
Many calls white black and say the sun sets in the east.
On many facades shallow, pretentious, icy smiles,

A world of quid pro quo, kindness real but rare.
There are beggars and thieves on the street of Paris and London, like Lagos and Soweto.
Here hatred mingles with love in the human tales.
The wild white west is another abode of man.
It's a land of whitewashed lies, tales and identities.
As the lot of men world over, so is the wild white west.

Compressive Ambivalence

My mind is in constant internal compressive ambivalence, caused by two opposing strong forces.

Every Nigerian especially those abroad who have tasted the beauty of a structured social democracy that works for the well-being of its citizens is plagued with a degree of mental affliction. I am referring to those who cared about the progress of the country they could call theirs, where their ancestors were buried, and where they hoped to spend their last days. Those that love the country not because the country is worth loving by virtue of her investment in them but for the fact that that is the country of their birth and the home of their loved ones and the only one, they truly have.

Many British when called upon for a service that demands a level of sacrifice: "For Queen and country", would be their response. In the United State, the equivalent might be: "*ad Deum patriae et familiae*" (For God, country, and family). These are demonstrations of patriotism in countries that have empowered their citizens. In Nigeria, the average citizen is a visa away from going away. The country is pushing her own away, even killing some for demanding that the country they call their home be made better, so they won't go away. The Lekki massacre is a point of reference. I cried throughout that night like a child. That was the day the patriotism of many youths was completely killed and the beginning of my nation-induced mental stress.

My mind is in a constant state of internal compressive ambivalence occasioned by two opposing forces pushing into it from opposite directions. There is this push I'm getting from my country which is trying to shove me away into some other part of the world, away from her incurable madness resulting from political prebendary which has resulted in an irredeemable corruption.

This has led to impregnable poverty, deadly insecurity, and many other miseries. I will set my description in a plane so you could picture it. We will assume this force is acting from my right-hand side. On the other hand, there is another force acting on me, opposite this force from the left-hand side. This is the force of racism, mistreatment, and challenges I am facing abroad just because of my race and nationality. These are acting together to tell me that I am not welcome. They are pushing me back home to my country of birth.

Imagine being placed at a spot on a highway and two lorries rammed into you from opposite directions at full speed at the same time. How do you survive such compressive forces and impacts? You will be pulverised and crushed.

Many a time when I am home alone, taking inventory of all that I have gone through during the day in a foreign country just because of my country of birth, and reading the news of what is coming out of that country, my mind suffers a great constrictive tension, a state of squashing ambivalence that I don't know how to deal with. I give this analogy to friends when I am trying to explain this situation. I was a very outgoing kid. As a child when I encountered challenges out there as children often do, I would run home to the arms of my mother and my older siblings for support, comfort, and healing. And running home was always a delight. But in my country today, many a time, if you are frustrated abroad, you dare not run back home for that would be identical to amputating your leg because of a fractured toe.

As I think about this and knowing full well that there is no end in sight yet when the arms of my country will welcome her own unto a comfortable embrace, my mind continues to suffer and at times the distress this causes liquifies into tears.

I know this is the case with many other people whose countries have no regard for the pains of their citizens. But one of the benefits of this is that it has helped me to develop mental resilience.

But where do we go from here? I think empathy and love for others will be very helpful. Seeking help for a mental health issue is cool. And then even if the world is falling on our shoulders as it often does, hope for better days ahead is very vital. Will that day ever come when I will truly say *ad Deum patriae et familiae* and mean it? I hope it comes soon enough.

About the Author

Joseph Ovwemuvwose is a budding scientist seeking to combine science, technology and art to develop solutions to some of the critical challenges facing the world. He is currently studying for his doctorate at Imperial College London. He has a master's degree from the University of Nottingham and a bachelor's degree from the University of Benin. He writes poems to give visibility to his thoughts on the issues that he cares about. Joseph Ovwemuvwose currently lives in London.

Printed in Great Britain
by Amazon